Random Dying Patterns

Aaron Harbour

(unproofed draft version)

Et al. Publications

Introduction

Let's say it's the end of the day, a beautiful day. A visiting new friend, conversations firmly lodged in the outside-of-the-ordinary laced with another chance to retell oft-told or over-told stories to each other without the desperation to impress sometimes tied to narration. He heads on his way across the country; I'm at a booth, dimmer than the rest of the bar, with a good beer and a little time on my hands to try again to restart this thing.

It becomes a matter of stealing time, a messy reallocation of resources. I'd love to say there was some kind of logical maximization process via which this hobby was exchanged for *that*. There seems to be too much time on offer – otherwise I'd be less prone to losing hours rewatching favorite shows, playing irredeemably unproductive games, risking a scroll through the comments below a minimally divisive news article, sleeping in regularly etc. There is also somehow too little time – how can I manage my responsibilities to others (often as a facilitator to their practices) with my own desire to produce? How can I leverage time which could be spent in near proximity to my loves which breath against those inanimate habits which give me the reason to do so myself?

These long book projects feel stolen. I've stolen the chance to bumble about ideas in broad daylight.

Unto whom is cast this shadow, whose inner ear finds coiled within the vibrations of my voice, whose eyes grow weary – driven in an orderly left-right across the page, so unnatural a rhythm for a sense trained on rapid redirection?

Short answer: A series of recollections, anecdotes, researchings etc.; each plot (collectively and as individuals) their inclusion, their process of overcoming edits and omissions. The result is the following text.

Longer answer: this started simply enough: a book about ghosts. Which I don't believe in, not even a little bit. But the process, which seemed well-enough calculated to produce a finished product, ran aground or else presented too many potential off ramps, detours, alternative routes.

But how to continue? When I used to make music, the slightest step forward (a finished song cycle, a small show etc.) would trigger a week or more of inactivity. Files ignored, time usually spent working on my project piddled away doing not much of anything. Having published the last of the quintet of roughly tied-off bits, which I intended to form if not the bulk of at least a solid first third of this project, I found myself firmly blocked, unable to commit anything but a random personal anecdote or two to the page. And these anecdotes grew more plentiful over time while the tons of texts I had read in preparation/research for this project grew ever more remote, gists forgotten without resorting to a pained backtrack through notes and pdfs long unopened.

My days are more or less joyful, inspiring; I lead a happy life, a fulfilling one. Yet a distemper colors it all – some distrust in life's constantness. That scene in *Pee Wee's Big Adventure* (Burton, 1985) : amidst a lengthy adventure to find his stolen bicycle (made lengthier by a fortuneteller directing him to venture to San Antonio, Texas – my home town) Pee Wee Herman walks by a pet store on fire. An animal lover and generally good person, he rushes in, assesses the situation, and begins to rescue all of the animals. He pauses at an aquarium full of snakes and moves on to the dogs, the cats, birds, fish, each time returning and delaying saving the snakes. The fire grows, the store is filling with smoke; with one last effort he runs in. We see a shot from the outside – Pee Wee runs out, both hands full of snakes, and faints.

I often use 'the snakes' as a descriptor for that thing you just can't bring yourself to do till it is almost too late. Taxes are 'the snakes', making a difficult phone call can be 'the snakes' et al.

It is a tension between knowing you have to do something and a marked inability to do the damn thing, a pressure that only grows as the situation becomes direr. And doing the damn thing, whatever it is, provides no real relief – there is no pleasurable release, feeling of satisfaction at having done something hard. Rather, a gentle nausea lingers and hopefully fades; or, as likely, the next 'snakes' queue up to be procrastinated, stressed about.

A second, related feeling – the 'I didn't do my homework' feeling: kinda self-explanatory but for instance I'm on a train right now headed to a place where a continued lack of success despite best efforts has put me in a position where the best case scenario is avoiding conversation on the matter and holding within a pained inadequacy, guilt.

These both crept about beneath my skin, hampering progress, making especially adhesive the grip of the ever-accessible internet and its boundlessness.
Inacurate/dishonest – pretending the pseudo-infinite of the browser window is wherein I loose my way when such a limited group of sites make up my daily travels.
Counting them (I know, I know, another excuse for procrastinating but at least I've the honesty to make this sham-labor public) I get twenty main websites for reading stuff, less than a dozen for hunting music, one main social media channel, six or so email tabs at a maximum, two minimum. This small bouquet of websites is more than enough to eat away the hours. A game of chess, some scrolling on Facebook, a refresh of the news sites (music and political) etc. and voila! Not much done.

Once I finally cracked open the four-part blog post meant to serve as a base for this book, months past real work on the thing and with a self-imposed deadline lurking on the horizon, the general jumble of it all couldn't help but give me license to carry on what I'd began. There is an indulgence in these chapters whether they be (relatively) deeply researched dives into an author's work, or anecdotes of fading accuracy (since when did these tales seem worth telling outside of late nights with a loved one, long drives with friends etc.?)

The first blog post began honestly enough

> "Apologies in advance: these are a few random limbs of a longer project. Initially planned to focus on ghosts and ghost stories in fiction, but the project has strayed and I fear will continue to do so."[1]

Funny how this attempt to give me some modicum of leeway to the project set the stage for an unraveling. No matter: herein reside these initial texts in all their unsettledness allowed in their retelling to go even more astray.

Okay, so it's not going to be all about ghosts, all about anything really. How could it be? When, not to mention the leaking in of both my own shit and the world directly astride me, there are so many attractive detours, red herrings, non-sequiturs etc. clamoring/clambering for my attention?

I wrote 'clammering'; spell check gives me clamoring and clambering – both seem to apply? Clamor – loud and insistant; clamber - an awkward and laborious climb or movement. I wish to split the difference. Or to say both in a single word, to say both and maybe a little more.

Finding one's self imbedded in the world's relentlessness and then noticing those productions, events, irregularities etc. which poke their head above the clouds, blasting off like rockets from the midst of it all. We watch these things rise and envy their accent; they each suffer only a few potential fates: they fail to reach escape velocity and gravity eventually reties them to the planet whole (landing) or otherwise (crashing), or they pull free of the grip of the planet and eventually we lose sight of them. Once free, ideas are unable to communicate the way they found release; we are left guessing why this or that achieves any kind of permanence.

I make jokes now and then about the ease of use and overuse of memory as a subject matter for art, especially as presented half-baked in artist and curatorial statements. But here we are, at the beginnings of a long text (or just beyond the beginning? Who's to say where this passage will come to rest), and it would be disingenuous for me not to claim that very tired term as a pediment of the construction before us. And, similarly hackneyed, mortality hovers in the air like a thick fog, a moist obfuscating mass which damns these proceedings with necessary self-importance.

'Too many notes' – the mock complaint against Mozart in *Amadeus* (Forman, 1984) feels a completely relevant charge against my type of ramble; I feel the occasional

---

[1] The original blog posts live at

need to condense my 'too many words' and it is not out of some genius 'just right' Goldilocks ambition or self-esteem that I continue to write. I recognize these words as far from ideal. Too hot or too cold, too soft or too hard.

In *Amadeus,* the jealous composer Salieri devises a way to destroy his too-talented rival: become the specter of Mozart's unsatisfied father, demanding work just beyond what is safely possible, draining him of his very life in the process. To affix the efforts of one's nemesis onto a single point, letting the sheer weight of their powers collapse upon itself is an admirably dark project. Outwardly he must maintain the appearance of being better than Mozart while internally he never doubts that his own music career will forever pale in comparison.

I think I'm more Salieri – I read plenty and recognize in the works of other authors a spark lacking in my own practice. Good but not great, though undeterred from doing things by this knowledge. But instead of leveling a 'too many notes' charge against the authors I can't help but admire, I jam these pages with notes, counter melodies that go nowhere, extraneous harmonics etc. I had for a second considered just starting, carrying on as if this was both introduction and first chapter but instead I'll dive in, now.

---

https://openspace.sfmoma.org/?s=aaron+harbour

Expect the ghosts to take their time to appear, endless distractions to grab my attention and pen. Expect them to get lost in the rush of distractions. I'll call each of the original parts by a letter, with a fifth section finishing the thing. Each will be expanded upon as I go, cleaned up a bit, invaded by new thoughts. Maybe it is a weird instinct but I can't help but thank you for giving this your time. *Thank you*. Onward.

A.

1. *Block*

It is a mistake to assume there are specialists and there are laymen on opposite sides of a room like boys and girls at a middle school dance, alien to each other, speaking different languages. In a general sense, this is sort of true: there are those who really know game theory or how to make a good pastry dough and everyone else. But more often than not there is sort of spectrum, maybe not between in-the-know and oblivious but between those for whom a given subject is complete gibberish (and more than that – completely uninteresting), then a range of individuals at different levels of semi-understanding and possibly extreme curiosity, not fully invested in a given subject but never the less interested peripherally in its basic principles and advances, and finally authorities on a given subject who amongst themselves would rate and rank each other's proficiency along a tighter continuum. Here I sit, loose-footing, at the base of any scale of expertise, lost as how to continue.

Mental torpor. Staring at the page, drawing up another browser over it for a minute wherein nothing new has occurred on any of its many tabs, minimizing it, bringing back that stinging whiteness, bare save the bad UI design of Word and these very lines (as yet not adjoined to other text).

Music (both hunted for and stumbled upon) continually leaps from elsewhere onto my hard drive and into my ears. Useful whether to distract me from progress or its lack; possibly to drive me forward if only a few steps. I've it on shuffle... my preference is a handful of artists/albums/genres conducive to the kind of half-distracted process I employ, but occasionally some other thing surfaces, altogether less musical, less familiar. Robert Barry produced an album for an exhibition at the Van Abbemuseum. Long pauses filled with record crackle and general ambiance punctuated by a voice:

....

....

....

.... Here it is

.... Nonsense

.... Inevitable

.... Deny

.... Sometimes

.... Touching

.... Endless

.... Understand

.... Too much

.... Of course

.... Please

.... Only one

....

....

.................[2]

A loaded pause between each fragment.

A peal of silence, a roar, an onslaught, a blitz; a crashing of silence, a calamitous silence.

What shakes me, what makes me hurt?

---

[2] From Robert Barry's *Otherwise* published by the Van Abbermuseum in 1981.

2. Intermezzo

> To-day we have ceased to be consciously afraid
> of the unseen;–knowing that we ourselves are
> supernatural,–that even the physical man, with
> all his life of sense, is more ghostly than any ghost
> of old imagining: but some dim inheritance of
> the primitive fear still slumbers in our being, and
> wakens perhaps, like an echo, to the sound of
> that wail in the night.
> —from "Ululation," in *In Ghostly Japan* by
> Lafcadio Hearn

Imagine a dim, quiet street — a disheveled, long
uninhabited mansion, lightless, arranged (curtains drawn,
angles just-so) such that no exterior glow manages to slip
in and find purchase upon its walls.

*A shadow made of smaller shadows butted against one
another puzzle-like. A congregation of shadow, a pod, a
murder.*

A black hole, standing with the door open (you've a key,
it was unlocked or whatever) you are on the threshold
staring in. A creaking as the building cools, materials
contracting slightly and pulling against one another;
perhaps a cat and/or mouse scuttle about in a distant
chamber. Imagine turning around, facing the street, your
back to the gaping maw of the thing. Step backwards into
the void, carefully, pull the door closed before you, close
your eyes.

A blinding darkness, strikingly dark, glaringly black, an obscenity of formlessness...

3. Without concession to humanity

What is a ghost? Let's ignore the experience of seeing a ghost. Let me explain: I have not seen one, I do not believe in them no more so than I believe in Gods etc. So, in total my knowledge of ghosts is as stories I've read, or stories told to me. Whether my interlocutor was genuinely under the impression they had seen a spirit or they were simply relating fiction, my personal experience has always been in the form of language. A story is told, whether hundreds of years ago in a play, in a recent novel, or person-to-person over a campfire. Truth or truthiness are not the point, evaluating the intention of the story teller is boring or impossible (or as likely both). Rather it is something in the telling, in the loose way in which the tale situates itself amidst the world we know, just slightly akilter and capable of infecting the world outside itself with that same sense of misaligned potential.

It is as if a pain can be so acute that it folds in and then out of itself, like the matter of stars imploding into a point carrying all the mass of the original but somehow now a cypher, simultaneously dark and radiant. Ghosts are a kind of temporal slant rhyme, a near-repetition in denial of the normal progress of things.

Trauma at its most severe refuses to fade away, becomes chronic. *Chronic* — meaning something that reoccurs (versus something *acute*). It gained its vaguely disapproving/pejorative connotation with regards to disease and addiction in the seventeenth century, but at its heart it is simply something of time, from Latin *chronicus* and Greek *kronikos* "of time, concerning time."

What doesn't concern time, what isn't time concerned with, what can be said to be *a*chronic? Perhaps what is meant is there are some things (somethings?) which engage in a looping, a repetition and then there are those things that do not. This text, this beer, this evening, a roll of toilet paper etc. will come to a definite end; sometimes hiccups feel like they might never.[3] Time is cleaved in two — time as the medium through which entropy and disorder increase and time as something eternal. What is chronic is adjoined to the latter.

Hauntings are chronic occurrences. In Lord Lytton's *The Haunted and the Hunters, or, The House and the* Brain, the skeptical main character challenges someone's fear of a haunted house, occupying it with his dog to figure out what is going on, believing a paranormal connection causes gives spectres their agency.

> "I will tell you what I would do. I am convinced from my own internal feelings that the small, unfurnished room at right angles to the door of the bed-room which I occupied, forms a starting-point or receptacle for the influences which haunt the house;

---

[3] Hiccups do not have this effect on me — I've the strange ability to stop them as soon as I notice I have them. Indeed, as often someone else notices I have them, informs me, and — voila — they are gone. Least useful of potential superpowers.

and I strongly advise you to have the walls opened, the floor removed,—nay, the whole room pulled down. [...]"

"And you think, if I did that—"

"You would cut off the telegraph wires."[4]

Eventually he returns to the house and uncovers some charmed personal effects hidden by a previous owner who met a tragic demise; they are disposed of and the spell is broken, "a quieter, better-conditioned house could not be found in all London."[5] The temptation that such a simple formula can break the spell, 'cut off the telegraph wires' is understandable but for something so inscrutable to be fell by simple logic seems lazy. Hauntings, like memory, should refuse such programmatic destruction.

Take a moment: recall something painful. Resolve: I'll forget this *now*, I'll destroy this pain, *now*. It will remain, perhaps with the memory of this futile effort in tow, perhaps more deeply ingrained. We can no more cease breathing, stop our hearts cold.

Likewise, spectres are at their core the embodiment of the unruly nature of reminiscence. I think all the time of this fragment of Kafka:

---

[4] Lytton, Edward Bulwer Lytton. *A strange story: to which is added, the haunted and the haunters.* Boston: Little, Brown, 1897.
[5] Ibid.

'But then he returned to his work as if nothing had happened.' That is a saying which sounds familiar to eus from an indefinite number of old tales, though in fact it perhaps occurs in none.[6]

Consigned to the grave, ghostly individuals return to their story "as if nothing has happened"; nothing so severe as to disengage them from their pursuits. But they are not as they were — now as nightmarish apparitions, or simply a nuisance to the living, any direct action is stymied. The tragedy which refuses spirits rest beneath the soil, the injustice they seek to right is exaggeratedly intractable in this state of neither-here-nor-there — frustratingly so. In the case of a haunting, having to witness loved (or loathed) ones move on without the ability to participate beyond the occasional rattled chain or unsettled family pet; watching the reoccupation of the site of their demise with such callous indifference to history by an unaware new tenant etc. must hurt; that they act out seems more than reasonable in this light. Cultural theorist Tiina Kirss describes how:

> [...] paradoxically, the poetics of haunting provides a richly metaphoric repertoire of conceptual tools which, if used with caution and sensitivity, can enable more precision about

[6] From the collection of little fragments and allegories titled *Reflections on Sin, Pain, Hope and the True Way* in: Kafka, Franz. *The Great Wall of China: Stories and Reflections*. New York: Schocken Books, 1970.

those interstices and intervals where
remembering happens.[7]

Or I think quite appropriately they can unsettle
misconstrued certainties, suggesting a separate path from
the much-lauded "acceptance."

Ghosts activate/occupy the disjuncture between worlds.
They do not connect two shores like a bridge creating an
easy pathway. Rather, visible in a spectrum between
states, ideas, etc., they *take up residence*, squatters in their
former home, homesteaders in the land of their birth.
These pains and frustrations on both sides of the border
between here and the hereafter offer us a chance to think
about the land of the living, our choices, our empathy and
the failure in all of these. Elsewhere in the same
compilation of odd riddles and phrases Kafka notes:

> There are questions which we could never get over if
> we were not delivered from them by the operation of
> nature.[8]

But this delivery seems insufficient, too easy a way out.

Let's talk about death, loss, pain, jealousy, regret. Horror,
real horror, and terror are maybe the rarest emotions we
feel. Felt briefly, as either their cause is quickly proved

---

[7] Kirss, Tiina. *Haunted Narratives*. Toronto: University of
Toronto Press, 2013
[8] Kafka, Franz. *The Great Wall of China: Stories and
Reflections*.

unfounded or the opposite and: snap: our necks are broken, sides split open, we are frozen, we drown. Horror can lead to any of the preceding feelings but somehow it maintains a distance from them, the difference between what presages and what comes to pass.

4. These times

Some lazy déjà vu.

It is as if I've sat here before - I have. I frequent this place
and doubtlessly have sat in essentially the same place as I
am in now, with a beer to my right, salt and pepper
shakers (moved out of the way of the laptop screen)
standing like sentries to the left, a crumble of napkin
present to daub ale from my beard, some old coasters
rounding out my company upon the table. Probably
wearing the same outfit, probably frequently escaping
this screen to view another silently broadcasting the
game.

*Mundanity encroaching herein when there was intimated
something more profound; badly disguised behind an excess
of literary device.*

Though the stage remains the same, each time I follow
the blocking and hit my mark before the footlights, the
performance has grown a bit since last time. Words have
been interspersed here and there, punctuation added or
removed, parts rearranged. I've returned to my work
similar to who I was when I made it, but much has
happened in the intervening days; I am not the same, if
only subtly so. It has been a tough duration certainly;

these times have left a mark.

Exacerbated by current events which bump into each other on their way to dishearten, death feels far closer than comfortable to the tip of my tongue on a regular basis. There was a time when a half-joking 'who died recently' felt an appropriate way to come up with a punny name for a pub trivia team. Not now, not while wallowing in a too-steady stream of tragedies both public and personal.

Having started out with a subject at an arm's length from the every day and now finding myself midstream trying to think about death, trauma, etc. in a general sense when the specific and close-to-home is all around has become difficult, has stymied me a bit. But maybe this is fair, more than fair. Misfortune has never taken a break; it metes out its productions at a constant clip; it is only my attentiveness to the calamitous as amplified by its proximity to me that shifts.

These particular recent months stung. Is the particular acuity of that sting an indictment of a failure of empathy, death of the non-famous or non-familiar failing to register an emotional affect? Surely, but the bite is no less sharp.

But here I am again, 'as if nothing happened', trying to speak. Language is a weak tool, like a prop rubber hammer to which more damage is done by the nail one is trying to embed. The more I type, the less certain I become. To what extent is this more than a gesture, something beyond just an accumulation of phrases?

In Tony Morrison's *Beloved* a group of women attempt the perilous act of exorcism "the voices of women searched for the right combination, the key, the code, the sound that broke the back of words."[9] I can hardly expect like Bane — having chosen not to eliminate but rather to disable Batman — to simply break language's confidence, its spine.

More reasonable goals: giving language a bit of an itch, making words yawn inconveniently. Revealing smaller verities in the form of hints. Or simply floundering in turns of phrase, anecdotal, spinning my wheels. Some truth revealed in the aftermath.

---

[9] Morrison, Toni. *Beloved: a novel.* New York: Knopf, 1987. To be discussed in depth later, maybe — it is a beautiful, dense, and painful text.

5. *A surprise*

A surprise — after a night devoid of clouds which might've obscured or refracted a clear view of a significant full moon, upon walking out of my door this morning the world is enrobed in a thick, atypical fog.

It is hard to imagine experiencing this stuff and not thinking there's an æther between all things. Water and nothing more, yes, but so fine a stuff, suspended among us, swirling at times, and still as a cube of aerogel at others. In a sense, yes, a medium between all: atmosphere without which we'd perish. It is the whims of this substance — density, temperature — wherein vapor gains temporary dominion on our altitude in quantities enough to obscure sight.

6. Indices

Maybe sometimes when we forget we really do forget, in a strict sense — an idea or image slips irretrievably away, the pattern of neural activity through which it is recalled is overwritten or scrambled somehow beyond retrieval. In the digital realm although algorithms are in place as checks and balances to stave off such forgetting, sometimes, due to consequences ranging from physical imperfections in the recording media to quantum effects, a bit will flip, changing from a one to a zero.

But just as often what is forgotten is merely misplaced, de-indexed. The matrix of sensations making up a past scene remain intact, but the connection between these and cognition, recall etc. is broken. The keys to a particular room are jumbled; the memory might return when unexpected, some background coincidence reconnecting the mislaid sequence to the whole. It may feel as if it returns for no reason whatsoever, suddenly an incident from grade school that you would have struggled to conjure upon request leaps upon the mental stage.

Equally inconvenient are those thoughts, memories, etc. that are *over*-indexed. Tied both to specific triggers and to esoteric, hard-to-pin-down ones, they foreground themselves despite effort, if not to forget, to not allow these shadows so imposing and constant a presence in one's life.

When again, in this nook of the bar suitable for a dozen but occupied by only me, these sentences feel ever more alien. A Pixies album blares in my ears; between songs the bar banter and whatever the bartender has chosen as background music slips in and is quickly erased. "Cactus" comes on.

This same spot saw at least a dozen at a birthday party recently. Saw me seven years ago awkwardly surrounded by semi-strangers on a trivia night. I knew it was a thing; I took my seat early and pretended to be incidentally in place as the crowds arrived and jostled for seating to play. Eventually I'd attach myself to that group, most would disappear but some would become not only constant teammates weekly but close friends, a new love would be leveraged against their willingness to accept this ritual and their potential efficacy as part of the team.

You'll have a collapse, but there's nothing in it, and you'll ask yourself...

Shuffle takes me back to the Robert Barry:

....
....
....
.... _Loved_
.... _Beyond_
.... _Forget_
.... _Doubt_
.... _Ourselves_
.... _Every so often_
.... _Describe_
.... _Obvious_
.... _Apart_
.... _Absent_
.... _Beautiful_
.... _Quietly_
.... _Realize_
.... _Attention_
.... _Stop_
.... _Terrible_
.... _Impossible_
....
....
....

Here the words change, bring their own charge, but the silence feels eerily familiar, echoes. Like the final moments of the disintegrated loops of William Basinski, the long gaps between sounds allow the world to leak back in while simultaneously sharing the subtle atmosphere of the media upon which it was recorded. And the condition of the specific copy — for a brief stretch a sharp click strikes a little over every half-second until the mar on the topology of the record is past. I'm reminded — I put on a loop, 'd|lp 6'.

While in college, William Basinski began playing with tape, inspired by both his musical upbringing and the experimental music program there. It was in school that he fell in love, moving to San Francisco for a bit then settling in Brooklyn. Musicians typically work on far more music than is ever released, and the same goes for recordings — a combination of demos, concert tapings, practice studio recordings, etc. piling up over time. These recorded matters are usually stored, and often a musician will go years before pulling out the old tapes or hard drives to listen to earlier works, if ever. It is not uncommon for an artist to produce more recorded material than could be reasonably listened to in several years.

Taking one's music from one format to another, often from an analog physical media to a digital one, is a process that in most instances takes considerable time or at least an amount of time greater or equal to the amount of tape being archived. The process typically involves simply playing it all and taking the sound from the playback into a computer through an interface of some kind. It can be exceedingly tedious as one cues up each bit and tries to get the cleanest, nicest re-recording. And the archive of files or tapes is always at risk as having been corrupted during storage.

In September of 2001, Basinski embarked upon what so many before him had done and began to digitize a bunch of his earlier work recorded on tape in loops. To his initial dismay, the material was failing. As the tape passed over the tape head, bits of magnetic material began to crumble and fall off of the substrate, and with them, the sound recorded there.

The material was forgetting, erasing itself in real time, and Basinski kept recording the tape loops as they fell apart, adding reverb and some small sound. What begins as a full but brief piece of music starts to fade in places, gradually, irreversibly, till little remains but bursts of sound and the warm noise of raw tape.

"The first thing I did was get cigarettes," says Basinski, recounting the day he watched the Twin Towers fall from atop his Brooklyn loft.[10] "My friend and I had just quit smoking," he continues, "but here we were, searching for five-year-old cigarette butts. I thought, 'The world's ending. We're going to have some real cigarettes.' So I got them, went back home, and there was chaos on the TV. We turned that off and turned on the music." Basinski

[10] Remaining quotes from *Self-Titled Magazine*, October 30, 2012, *The Self-Titled Interview: William Basinski* by Andrew Parks.

had recently wrapped his *Disintegration Loops* series, so he cranked the volume, cracked open the windows and went up to his roof, where he noticed a friend across the way, who had a video camera out.

"It was the last hour of daylight," says Basinski, "so I asked her to help me frame the camera and let the tape run out. It was just devastating."

The works became inextricably linked to that event, with stills from the video made that day used as covers for the releases, parted out over time before being released as a box set. The *Disintegration Loops* are breathtaking, elegiac, and meditative. Death, memory, entropy, time... subjects which tend to be addressed in tedious, overindulgent manners find themselves evoked by a work which simply follows a process to its natural end without force. Here were ghosts visible on the breach between worlds.

From abstraction to matter and back again.

These albums, these reveries, these *rememories*...

Let's get more specific.

B.

1.

> But before he could determine the question,
> though not the faintest motion of the air in this
> infinite waste of wasteless light was manifest, the
> door that he had left ajar behind him had,
> unperceived by Mr. Asprey, already begun to stir
> upon its hinges. There sounded a tiny click in the
> supreme silence. He turned his head. Too late,
> again! — the door was shut. And since between
> heaven and earth there followed not the remotest
> hint of an approaching kloop-kloop of hoof or
> muffled clatter of wheel, it looked as if he must
> be intended to walk. So he set out.

— Walter de la Mare, *The House*[11]

A weight lifted: having submitted the first batch of words
and seen them published online, I can sally forth a little
lighter in the saddle. And so much already half-thought,
half-written sits waiting to be drawn from for these
subsequent portions! Comfort in the first step taken,
however haphazard.

Should I eschew metaphor, focus on discreet examples,
avoid straying from the source, the text? Or else the
opposite, get strange, meander.

---

[11] De La Mare, Walter. *Best stories of Walter De La Mare.* London: Faber & Faber, 1983. Out of fairness it must be said this bit's sentiment is well enough expressed in the introduction, but as I like the phrasing I've saved it from the 'command+Z'.

Or do as I've done: hedge, try to do both, never really investing in either; trail off when convenient, change the subject when it becomes obvious an element is at loggerheads with the broader project. As if I can help it; onward.

2. Sweep my grave when I'm gone

Then first to the pilgrim's gaze the steeps
revealed their nakedness; — and a trembling
seized him, — and a ghastly fear. For there was
not any ground, — neither beneath him nor
about him nor above him, — but a heaping only,
monstrous and measureless, of skulls and
fragments of skulls and dust of bone, — with a
shimmer of shed teeth strown through the drift
of it, like the shimmer of scrags of shell in the
wrack of a tide. [...]

"I cannot," cried the pilgrim, trembling and
clinging; "I dare not look beneath! Before me and
about me there is nothing but skulls of men."

"And yet, my son," said the Bodhisattva, laughing
softly, — "and yet you do not know of what this
mountain is made."

The other, shuddering, repeated: — "I fear! —
unutterably I fear!...there is nothing but skulls of
men!"

"A mountain of skulls it is," responded the
Bodhisattva. "But know, my son, that all of them
ARE YOUR OWN! Each has at some time been
the nest of your dreams and delusions and
desires. Not even one of them is the skull of any

other being. All, — all without exception, —have been yours, in the billions of your former lives."
— Lafcadio Hearn, *A Fragment*[12]

The sense that behind and before me are skulls of individuals terribly similar to myself. So much so that me having been, breathed, loved, lived, is 'neither here-nor-there'. This is a nightmare which perhaps strikes especially hard those (self-?)charged with being among those that both consume *and* make. Are we trapped in a loop, endlessly repeating the same gestures? Or, at least equally terrifyingly, are we truly bringing the new into the world only to have it scuttled along with everything else in time's relentlessness?

A practical joke by prank phone caller Longmont Potion Castle goes awry: having posted online a Super Nintendo at a low price he calls a thirteen-year-old named Tim who paged him. He is too late: Tim has already purchased a game system, yet the prankster persists (very much in keeping with his style), offering it for five dollars and fifty-nine cents should Tim manage to scrounge up the money (from his lunch money, trading his CDs or toys for the machine etc...) and make across town. Eventually, Tim is coerced into talking about his life and his general dissatisfaction:

[...] LPC: Do you like anything about school?

---

[12] Hearn, Lafcadio. *In ghostly Japan*. Boston: Little, Brown and Co., 1899.

Tim: No.

LPC: Do you like your parents?

Tim: Sort of.

LPC: What is about your parents you like and what is it
about your school you don't like?

Tim: *Many things.*

LPC: What do you plan to be when you grow up?

Tim: I plan to be dead when I grow up.

LPC: How long from... how long... how long, until the final
day... or have you planned that far?

Tim: I haven't planned that far... probably around 18, 21

LPC: When I was 14, I did not think I'd live past 20... and here I am, 75.

Tim: You are not 75 years old.

LPC: I don't see why such a bright young man would want to end his life so soon...

Tim: I do.

LPC: Why is that?

Tim: *Because nobody'll miss me.* [...][13]

---

[13] The call continues; eventually the kid's father joins the call. It gets dark – full of LMPC's fake violent threats (culled from responses of recipients of his crank calls into a bit of a language of it's own) and the father's vaguely homophobic implications. The collapse of someone being entirely ridiculous and false with something so terribly real is hard to believe her. LMPC is an acquired taste, growing more powerful when consumed in bulk but this particular piece stands out as Give a listen. Part
1: https://www.youtube.com/watch?v=GJ7txuDfSHA
Part 2: https://www.youtube.com/watch?v=9W9CWFtTflc

Nobody will miss me us either, Tim.
Not for long anyway. The world will barrel forth bearing
neither our mark nor the noticeable void of our absence.
These are childish concerns, or else, lifetime ones which
at best goad one into making a difference and at worst
undermine motivations, ambitions.

The title of an oft-covered folk blues tune "See That My
Grave Is Kept Clean," sung beautifully by Blind Lemon
Jefferson among others, speaks to this desire — let
something remain once I am gone, don't forget me. But
by immortalizing these lyrics, death invades life and
survives its surrender.

Having died of an uncertain cause in Chicago, Jefferson's
remains found themselves nearly just that — forgotten,
taken back to Texas and interred in an unmarked grave
in a segregated cemetery. By 1996, the cemetery and
marker were in poor condition and a new granite
headstone was erected in 1997. In 2007, the cemetery's
name was changed to Blind Lemon Memorial Cemetery,
and his gravesite is kept clean by a cemetery committee in
Wortham, Texas.[14]

---

[14] From the wiki on Blind Lemon Jefferson. There are a large
number of blind blues musicians including Sonny Terry,
Blind Willie McTell, Blind Mammie Forehand, Blind Boy
Fuller, Blind Willie Forehand, Blind Blake, Blind Rosevelt
Graves etc. The concurrence of so many blind individuals in
an artistic field is hard to explain; the simplest answer
would be a virtuosic performance is all the more noteworthy
from someone with a disability however distanced from the

Yet the actual location of his burial will forever remain lost. And despite the late coming pride in the man, the new headstone, engraved with the lyrics

> *Lord, it's one kind* favor *I ask of you*
> *See that my grave is kept clean*

cannot help but point by exclusion to the countless other black people buried thereabouts, forgotten, lost to neglect, *unmissed*. This weird intervention of abstract human desire and the ambiguity between personal narrative and song lyric briefly escapes into the specific, physical world only to leave us with an unforgivable void.

> The legend tried to explain the inexplicable. As it came out of a substratum of truth it had in turn to end in the inexplicable.[15]

---

skill presented the disability is. This seems unsatisfactory, as does any idea that blindness makes the blues more acute. We're left with the enigmatic, coincidence. The wiki on blind musicians is worth perusing: https://en.wikipedia.org/wiki/Blind_musicians

[15] Kafka, Franz. *The basic Kafka*. New York: Pocket Books, 1979. An edition published when I was one and my father eighteen. Though he'd eventually lose himself to a combination of religion and politics, my dad had some good books, typical of a kind of fledgling thinking man of the late seventies — a vintage book of Poe's poems, a collection of pulp copies of Herman Hesse's books and this Kafka pocketbook (blue with thin green, red and gold stripes on the right side of the cover). In my preteens I'd sneak them away to read; the ideas in these slip into any attempts to think hard about things to this day and I suspect always will.

> Thinking 'bout my grandmama, find a bottle
> I'mma wallow when I lie in that
>
> I just want my time and my mind intact
> When they both gone,
> you can't buy 'em back
> Earl Sweatshirt, 'Grief'[16]

My grandmother on my mother's side died five years ago
– she was the person in the world I cared most about
which would be an awkward thing to say if anyone who
would feel jealous about such a claim thought otherwise
for even a second. Importance is not doled out in sync
with time spent – I lived with my grandparents for four
or five years and as much with first my father and step
mom and then my mom and step father but those first
bunch of years really took. When choosing (or thinking I
was choosing) to switch homes I was never really giving
up my grandma's as my real home base. Her voice, her
simple presence guided me. Functionally illiterate, always
cooking or cleaning, there would be little I could claim to
have in common with her yet her spirit, her capacity to
love my brother and I and her commitment to the task of
living with us, making a place for us to become who we'd

---

[16] From 'Huey' on the same album *I Don't Like Shit, I Don't Go Outside*

> I spent the day drinking and missing my grandmother
> Just grab a glass and pour up some cold white wine
> And a Colt 45 in it, you know how I get it

be for better or worse leaves me speechless to this day, meant so much.

This isn't to say those years spent with my grandparents weren't without difficulty – there was an intense sadness woven into my life there, revisited in the summer or on weekends when I'd go back: my grandmother had a strange relationship with alcohol and another side to her self which, when conjured was dangerous, hurtful – not physically, but nevertheless effective in its violence. Yet this weight never shook my grandmother's hold on my heart (or perversely aided its grip).

When she died I traveled back for the first and only funeral I've ever attended. Grief-stricken, eyes red from constant crying, I saw her lowered into her grave, a moment that felt like a tourniquet on my life in Texas – I've not been back since despite having much family still there that I miss and that misses me. Going back to Texas feels like the ultimate 'snakes'. I don't think much about Texas, not too much anyway, it rests in the back of my mind in a reserve of feelings alongside most of my youth. Inapplicable to the everyday save an anecdote or two now and then.

Then a bad day, a terrible week both socially and at work, the sole of one of my favorite shoes finally gives up, I forget the name and face of a long-time acquaintance making me feel like an asshole when they correctly point out 'we've met several times before'. For a dinner I was making I decide to cook my grandmother's recipe for beans. The one she was known for throughout both sides of my family, that I had a few times a week for years. Not a written recipe, not something she showed me how to make, but nevertheless they come out perfect.

Incommunicable joy.

4. Casper

There's no such thing as a ghost, not really anyway. Yet it is insufficient to classify ghosts or the supernatural as real or unreal. On the one hand, no, there is no afterlife, no strange way port between some specific beyond and the world of the living which, should one find one's self there, leaves a crack open through which contact can be made with those still breathing. Once one is no longer alive in the material world there is no method (however clumsy) of interacting with matter — turning on an unplugged TV, shaking a chair, making the air hot or cold in a specific spot in a house etc. Death brings the you that does things to an end, full stop.

Okay, but how should we balance truth against an obstinate idea? Given there is no afterlife, there is no such thing as a ghost. Sure, yet the afterlife resists so quick an internment — there is most certainly such a thing as a ghost, if only in the form of a persistent concept, an ancient meme of sorts, resistant to the slings and arrows of either science or logic. Ghosts as an idea are very much real — few if any cultures lack some form of spirits or ghost. Technological and social advances may have quelled some of the more extreme reactions to the supernatural (witch trials, etc.) but ghosts and their ilk remain a constant presence. An overused line seems relevantly paraphrased here: were ghosts not real it would be necessary to invent them.

When thinking about this subject it is the persistence of the concept across time which draws me to working in this way, digging through my memories of media and reading new-to-me works in an attempt to draft something which may serve as a basis for further investigation.[17] Which in a roundabout way brought me to Casper.

The first appearance of Casper, in *The Friendly Ghost* (1945), adapted by Bill Turner and Otto Messmer from an original story by Joseph Oriolo and Seymour Reit and directed by Isadore Sparber, begins with a narrator describing how

> There are some people who believe in ghosts, and there are some people who don't. If you are the 'believe in ghosts' kind, then, this story is about one. If you are the 'don't believe in ghosts' kind... well, this story is about one anyway.[18]

I'm of the latter kind; *these texts are about them anyway.*

---

[17] It is easy to imagine this or any number of false starts I've made eventually making up something of an introduction. Addicted to a hedge between deeply considered (by deeply I mean over the course of many half-awake mornings, showers, train rides) sequences of ideas and other portions improvised while sitting staring at the page, it's hard to say where this will begin and/or end.

[18] Credited as I. Sparber a.k.a. Isadore "Izzy" Sparber, who produced nearly 400 cartoons *after* a long period of going uncredited for his work.

In the world of these cartoons, being a ghost is an occupation/identity, distinct from whatever preceded being a spirit. But while Casper's fellow ghosts enjoy the art of scaring the living, Casper is different, he "would rather stay home and not frighten people" — he'd rather make friends.

The three original shorts share roughly equivalent narratives. In each, the ghosts awaken (by moonlight, after midnight, etc.) to go scare the populous and Casper ignores a fellow ghost imploring him to join the general frightening. The ghosts spread out to terrify and Casper wanders off to try to meet people, and to forget that he's a ghost.

He runs into a number of animals in each cartoon in his attempt to make friends – a rooster, a mole, a cat and the mouse it is chasing, a cow, a skunk, a turtle, a pelican (and the fish in his mouth), a flock of nesting ducks. He scares them all; Casper: "It's no use, I'm just a scary old ghost." He is so dejected that in the first cartoon Casper puts himself on a train track to commit suicide (to no avail — the train rolls right through him).[19]

In each, he meets someone not afraid of him, a young boy and girl, named Bonny and Johnny, a fox, and a duck and

---

[19] This second-level wish for death is a novelty I'll try to explore later. Primarily a humorous device, it also serves to highlight the fecklessness of the undead and the anguish this causes, along with the imposition upon ghosts of living-human feelings — a kind of zoe/*ero*-anthropomorphism.

they become quick friends. Someone threatens the new friend(s), but upon seeing Casper they are scared away. In *The Friendly Ghost* (1945), unafraid Bonny and Johnny bring Casper to a very alarmed mother who does her best to shoo away the ghost. As he is leaving, dejected, a banker comes asking for payment of the mortgage and threatening foreclosure. Casper frightens him to the point he rescinds all claim on the property.[20] In the second and third shorts, the threats are hunters and their dogs (fox and duck hunters respectively).

It is not enough to wish to not be alone — some other must accept one's invitation to friendship; that anyone will do so is not a given. The third short, *A Haunting We Will Go* (1949), begins with Casper in a school for ghosts, the chalkboard covered with clever slogans such as, "Boo unto other as you would have other boo unto you," "Fright makes right,' and "I will Spook when spoken to." Not going with his classmates to scare the populace, Casper unsuccessfully engages a bevvy of animals, remarking finally "I might as well be dead, nobody wants me for a friend."[21]

---

[20] The mom seeing this is thankful, and lets him be part of the family. Bonny, Johnny and Casper head off to school together in typical school clothes; it is hard to imagine his attendance going well. That the filmmakers choose to place bankers in the same category re: humans that hunters are re: hunted animals is telling.

[21] On par with Casper's oddly sad and funny attempted suicide, this desire for death by the dead is primarily an ironic device on the part of the writer simultaneously using and mocking our imposition on others, whether they are inanimate objects, animals, or the dead, of our zoe/ero-

Casper suffers from an excess of kindness and a desire to be around people — symptoms quite different from those typical of a ghost. I'm reminded of the Osamu Tezuka manga and anime character Unico.[22] A small, terribly cute unicorn, Unico is banished by the gods for bringing too much happiness — happiness which rivals the gods' own ability to shape the whims of mankind. The West Wind, charged with getting rid of Unico, shows pity and does her best to hide the creature. Unico wanders the forest, approaching animals and trying to befriend them ("Hi! I'm Unico! *Will you be my friend?*") Eventually those around Unico learn various lessons about kindness and its lack, but the intensity of his power is not without victims. In the second feature film, *Unico in the Island of Magic* (Murano, 1983) there is an evil magician, Lord Kuruku, who has taken it upon himself to rid the world of people, turning them into "living puppets," golem-like stone figures which then walk to Kuruku's castle to become its bricks — a castle made of people. Kuruku was once a marionette which eventually broke and was

---

anthropocentrism. An envisioning of the death-wish as a wish for specifically a death in an atheist universe of death-finalism.

[22] The Unico cartoons are obscure, yet at one time they leaked into the world via a home video release (when all kinds of material was being scrounged up to fill the video store aisles) and a presence on the nascent Disney Channel. They are terribly good — as are all the Sanrio-backed cartoons of the eighties. I recommend the dark "there's no going home" narrative *Ringing Bell* (Hata, 1978) https://www.youtube.com/watch?v=boNEUjQbGvg

thrown away. One way or another, Unico ends up facing off with him and it is Unico's boundless ability to love which wins the day — after a lengthy battle, Unico declares his fondness for Kuruku, his wish to be friends, his understanding... Kuruku is defeated; it was his hatred of mankind that was keeping him alive.

The violence of unfettered love upon someone too complicated to easily accept that burden— one can only wonder what fate Casper's banker would have met had Casper been given the time to properly attempt to make his acquaintance.

5. *Estuary*

After years of consistently gliding into my life, the bat
rays have not graced me with their presence. Annually,
early June, coinciding with a bursting into life of
thousands of smelt or other tiny schooling fish, the rays
would come, grey apparitions. A bridge walked over on
my way to work crosses an inlet from the Oakland
Estuary to Lake Merritt, concealing beneath a massive
pumping station which helps regulate the depth of the
artificial lake at the heart of the city, Tides draw water in
either direction through a grating which is biannually
cleaned of collected detritus and algae by a scuba diver.
When the water is heading out to the sea the base of the
bridge teems with life, including the aforementioned fish
along with those who enjoy eating them such as egrets,
night herons, cormorants, and the occasional crane. The
rays swim up against the grates, feeding on the freshly
spawned creatures filtering through. They thrash about,
in arms-reach should one walk down closer, their
undulating edges breaking the surface.

And though, after a spell of heat which sharpened to a
fierce point one Thursday just as the sea breeze returned
to comingle oppressive and ideal weathers in intermittent
waves, the more typical cool overcast mornings leading to
comfortable warm afternoons, the rays stayed away.

On the left are a series of administration buildings one of
which I work in; on the right is a large parking lot for the
Laney College Campus; ahead a highway glides by. In this

collection of lands there is an ambition to place a baseball stadium and its parking

On the water's edge Canadian geese breed along with a larger white variety. There are a few unlabeled bird shit and graffiti-stained plop sculptures as well. People fish along the banks, as often their prey is small fish to be taken elsewhere and used as bait. Recently I saw in the distance a man walking his large German Shepard, which took off running full speed with a gait completely different than the more familiar clipped gallop possible in a smallish dog park. I quickly realized its target: the flock of grazing geese and their children who, spotting this danger all started making their waddling way to the water, honking loudly while the man yelled equally loudly for his dog to stop. But something had kicked in deep within that dog, and much faster than the flightless goslings he caught up to a straggler and grabbed it by the neck, triumphant. He started to carry it back to the yelling man who told him to drop it; he did, started back to the man but then as quickly the dog ran back and picked back up the now struggling bird, carrying it a bit farther before finally dropping it and returning to his owner. They went on their way; the bird lay their, its extended family slowly gaining the courage to return to their scrabbling ground and maybe mourn a bit the unlikely to survive victim.

These strangely real life moments are common in this neighborhood near the water's edge. A night heron befriends an Asian grocery, hanging around where deliveries are made eating what it can and being occasionally treated to some thick pig skin tossed atop a box truck. Something so alien as these rays returning annually – their smoothly skating in from the sea for a few warm months. Until, all at once they didn't, leaving life a little more ordinary.

(Thursday, June 29th, 2017)

And then it happened. I left work early; crossing the bridge on the way to catch a train I looked down to the water as I always do. The water was flowing outward but gently so, and was clearer than normal – a combination of its relative stillness and the correct angle and amount of sunlight cutting through it. Some days the water races to sea, murky with jostled silt. On others it might be creeping perfectly along but a bright thin pall of clouds turns the surface to glass. But today it was perfect. I watched a cloud of small fish swarm to and fro, the sea plants swaying, gripping the grate. Suddenly I saw one, then more of my seasonal friends slither in. Four total, two small and two larger, like a family keen on summering in this outwardly unremarkable urban notch in the coast. Seeing them has given me a great deal of joy; a remarkable routine continues unbroken.

6. Another surprise

Hot days, more than usual, hot and dry. A band of under-twenties is playing something mistakable for heartfelt jazz at the bar. Usually confining themselves to mellow standards and covers of pop tunes (that easy pleasure of the moment of recognition — *it's The Cure, it's "Superstition"*), for this song they've drifted into some more challenging Miles Davis territory, they're getting kinda free with it. Afraid of offending anyone my headphones are off, at least until they finish this set. My beer is cold on this reasonable facsimile of an Indian summer evening. Everything seems a version, pastiche.

Home, a quick show or two gets watched and we fall asleep, me first but she not long after, the cat on her own schedule visits off and on the whole time. Then, for whatever reason we all awaken to find the world transformed – it is raining, rather hard; there is thunder and maybe lightning and half-awake this all feels dreamlike. I grew up with this type of storm-as-reward for a day spent baking uncomfortably. You could watch it brewing on the horizon, thunderheads rising along with the potential that they'd release upon the parched city a brash relief. But here precipitation seems uniquely indifferent; even this one instance of post-heat rain was mishandled by nature as it occurred late enough as to be missed by many who only learned later by friend's tales or social media that nature interjected herself into the normal chain of events. Had this sudden downpour happened closer to our near-solstice long evening not only would less have been fully and uninterruptedly asleep, we'd be even more likely to dive in – I can imagine dropping whatever I was doing and walking dumbly outside into the downpour. I miss storms, real weather.

But still... I shouldn't downplay the worth of being extra present a moment together with her, a bonus dash of intense real presence though quite quickly we're both back asleep. When we awaken, it takes a firm affirmation aloud of that rain to really let it sink in as having happened.

Surprise: the possible but improbable asserting an ambiguity underlying the ordinary stream of instances; making real for a while the potential for an even wilder branching off of the present into the future.

7. Eid ma clack shaw

One of the first tracks shared from the 2009
album *Sometimes I Wish We Were an Eagle* by Bill
Callahan was the curiously titled "Eid Ma Clack Shaw".
In it, two dreams escape the night's reverie, shaking free
of the line between fact and fiction, present and past,
present and wished-for present.

>Working through death's pain
>Last night I swear I felt your touch, gentle and
>warm
>The hair stood on my arms — how, how, *how*?
>
>Show me the way, show me the way
>Show me the way to shake a memory
>Show me the way, show me the way
>Show me the way to shake a memory
>
>I flipped my forelock, I twitched my withers, I
>reared and bucked
>I could not put my rider aground
>All these fine memories are fucking me down
>I dreamed it was a dream that you were gone
>I woke up feeling so ripped by reality
>Love is the king of the beasts
>And when it gets hungry it must kill to eat
>Love is the king of the beasts
>A lion walking down city streets
>I fell back asleep some time later on
>And I dreamed the perfect song

It held all the answers, like hands laid on
I woke halfway and scribbled it down
And in the morning, what I wrote, I read
It was hard to read at first but here's what it said:

"Eid ma clack shaw zupoven del ba
Mertepy ven seinur cofally ragdah"
"Eid ma clack shaw zupoven del ba
Mertepy ven seinur cofally ragdah"
Show me the way, show me the way
Show me the way to shake a memory [...]

The first verse involves a lost love. Whether via death or
as a result of infidelity by either of the couple,
estrangement is real, painful. His hair stands on end —
horripilation — this and other expressions mark our body
as a result of stimuli regardless of conscious efforts to
ignore, look past, forget.[23] Once awake, the present is
hard to accept in view of the fictive alternative. Callahan
gives a metaphor in which he is a horse and this
subconscious will/construction is a rider he is unable to
toss. Love is something which surpasses human agency.
When invoked (accidentally or otherwise) its whims defy
control, defy the finality provided by death.

---

[23] Horripilation — I've failed to find a word for a very
particular linguistic experience: a word's roots lead to its
spelling but also seem to hint at its eventual meaning.
Horripilation accidentally/incidentally implied horrification,
the process of being horrified, but in actuality has nothing of
the sort underlying it.

Death seems like a prank perpetrated by the world. Humans, so intent on imbuing themselves with devotions grand and mundane, can be met without warning by a demise which lays waste to any such purpose. Death invokes a purposelessness — yet this is surmountable, as it is almost inevitable that those left behind will regain the resolve to carry on.

In the second verse, a dream provides an eureka moment — the perfect song, which the narrator quickly jots down upon awakening. But once again the dream world has played something of a prank: reading back his half-awake scribblings, he realises it is essentially gibberish. Maria Fusco, discussing the art object in terms of a riddle, notes: "Criticism can cajole objects to speak, but we must be prepared to accept that these very same objects may only be able to answer us in riddles."[24] Likewise, inspiration may very well provide enigma.

The process of making this text is not dissimilar: I read, watch, taking bits and pieces and cutting them into various documents with various notes, half ideas or reasonings peppered throughout. But this past me has played a joke — upon opening the documents in a folder set aside for this project, some of them defy any logic. I have no idea what I meant, why I copied a specific quote, what I meant by my interjections, etc. These documents get reopened now and then to see if these communiqués

---

[24] Fusco, Maria. "Say who I am: Or a Broad Public Wink." *Circa Art Magazine*, October 8, 2010.

might not be deciphered; some texts find their way into the final work while others lay discarded, written by the sphinx-me of the past.

And there are times when the words come pouring out regardless of my access to a device or materials to record them. I stand in the shower or on a crowded train and suffer ideas one after the other, tripping over each other to foreground themselves.

Does blood, like some Marxist ideal, circulate throughout the body indifferent to where with its oxygen passenger in tow it travels? The same cells warming my fingertips, responsible for erections and the blush which strikes one having been complimented at random here in my dim booth.

Where do I sneak in that bit of Lil' Wayne's verse on Solange's 'Mad':

> Are you mad 'cause the judge ain't give me more time?
> And when I attempted suicide, I didn't die
> I remember how mad I was on that day
> Man, you gotta let it go before it get up in the way
> *Let it go, let it go*

Or the fragment "Look up *restorative justice*."

Or a document with only the observation:

A license plate surround that says 'HANG UP' on top and on bottom 'QUIT BEHAVING BADLY'

There are bits that, however disjointed, have felt strangely necessary to say long enough that I'll insert them, pretending they've enough weight to gain purchase upon the page (as opposed to disappearing, floating away). The following splits the difference between useless and completely unavoidable, a quick thought which recurred in my thoughts throughout this project's slow, disjointed, pained realization:

If there were ghosts I'd wish them access to who I am.

So many lies buttress the day-to-day. Oversights, purposeful omissions, misrepresentations — we mistell, mar otherwise sincere and true relationships with our self-design.

Were I to be damned let me be so by truth.

C

1.

Occasionally while waiting for a train underground, standing in the waiting area between the two tracks which stop at a given platform — one heading east and the other west or north/south — a third possibility will present itself. Suddenly the digital voice and red LED signs pronounce: this approaching train, whose roar you hear growing louder, *will not stop.*

Maybe for training or due to some internal system need for this particular machine to get to a starting point further down the line – the reasoning driving the vehicle down the track heedless to the demands of passengers waiting on the platform will forever remain unknowable.

And perhaps it will or won't decelerate a tiny bit as it flies by; perhaps one can just make out the pilot as the lead car swifts past. But regardless it doesn't stop, carries almost no one from a somewhere unknown to a second equally unknown elsewhere.

These phantoms produce a distinct kind of cold wind, pressing a column of air piston-like down the tunnel and out into the station. Not in the limited way a train intent on stopping does, coming closest to full force only at the very point it exits the tube into the grander volume of the platform but easing as the mass comes to a rest, opens doors...

Rather, these indifferent masses of metal and plastic drag with them a fierce wave of an alien atmosphere, wildly swirling like pilot fish struggling to keep up with their shark companion. A thrilling gust, a gale signaled by a distant rumble which builds in volume and force until the tail of beast slips past and the sound recedes. One hundred tons of matter hurling down the track.

It is here, on a bench, running late, coat zipped a little higher, where we rejoin our proceedings.

2. Ordinary ghosts 1

If the dead are stirred from their slumber by an excess (of innocence, pain, guilt, love, etc.) into arising as ghosts, is mediocrity the path to the beyond? Not the barely-beyond of those that haunt, but the beyond-beyond, the never to be heard from again?

The voices of the ghosts of the mundane dead are as barely audible as their stories are legible in the annals of history. We walk on the sand together looking for shells — each of the grains itself a shell or part of some creature's remains. But they are not what we mean by 'shells' when we say we are hunting for shells, rather we mean significant ones, bold shapes, bright colors, complete or if not so at least in very large pieces.[25]

Those grains of sand perhaps consisting of complete but microscopic shells of thing or bits of things so small as to become indivisible from the general clamor of particles are the stage upon which what we value settles – a full sand dollar, a conch, some portion of an oyster's interiorly oil-slicked former home, a distinctly stratified bit of rock etc.

---

[25] Sometimes the opposite is true. We love *our* cat, but at night on the same beach feral cats are seen trundling about on their own adventures and should one deign to respond to our 'Here Kitty-Kitty!'s and various snaps and non-verbal cajolings we will realize we love *cats* nearly as much as we love our own.

Nevertheless, while the truly tragic seem to have a stranglehold on the spectral, there are examples in fiction of ordinary ghosts — individuals whose minor tragedies (as all, or at least most deaths can be considered as such) and general dead-ness are enough to place them in some spiritual realm alongside Hamlet's father et al.

In *The Undertaker*, a short story by Alexander Pushkin, the titular character, an Adrian Prokhorov, feels slighted while attending a party. New to town, he was invited to a neighboring shoemaker's silver wedding anniversary. Those in other professionals seem to hold him and his at a remove — during a toast a police guard turned to Prokhorov, exclaiming (to the laughter of the crowd), "And how about you? Drink, brother, to the health of your corpses."[26] That labor involving the handling and interment of the dead would be felt apart from that which encompasses plumbing or law or brewing etc. should come as no surprise — it feels quite natural to think of that profession as grim. But to the undertaker, his is a task necessary to be performed for each and every person (in their due time) and thus is no less honorable. Having considered, prior to feeling looked down upon, inviting his neighbors and acquaintances over for a meal, he vows to instead give the same invitation to his customers — the dead.

[26] *The Undertaker* appears in: Pushkin, Alexander Sergeyvich. *The captain's daughter and other stories*. New York: Vintage Books, 2012.

He goes to sleep angry and a bit drunk, but is awakened with the news of a death, an old widow named Triukhina has died and dealing with this body is part and parcel of his catching up financially. He spends the day dealing with all the arrangements. Upon arriving home *they* have come... walking into his home the individuals he has buried in various states of decay have responded to his summons and confront him.

> "As you see, Prokhorov," said the brigadier in the name of the whole honorable company, "we have all risen in response to your invitation; only those stayed at home who are by now really incapacitated, who have entirely gone to pieces or have only their bones left without skin [...]"[27]

The Sergeant to which Prokhorov sold his very first coffin, at this point not much more than a skeleton, tries to embrace him, is pushed away, crumbles. The crowd is angered and rises against the undertaker when, in a flash, he awakens in bed; not only had his gathering of the dead not happened, so had not the funeral he thought he had prepared the day before.

The dead had not visited, but also he had not been rescued via profit on death. Prokhorov is left in the place his community wished him and his occupation — necessarily apart, neither dispensable nor ordinary,

---

[27] Ibid.

refused the right to certain ambitions by the nature of his profession.

We are not given any indication he has learned a lesson — there is no day after scene like Scrooge in *A Christmas Carol*. Scrooge, having seen the error in his ways via a ghostly visitation does his best to make things right immediately, transforming from miser to philanthropist.[28] Prokhorov's revelation offers no clear transformation. Assuming he takes his vision to heart, he is simply granted a renewed appreciation for the gravity of his vocation.

More often these bit player ghosts are on their way to some uncertain elsewhere, distinct from the subjects of most literature, trapped in the semi-here-and-now.

---

[28] From *The Muppet Christmas Carol* (Henson, 1992):
Narrator: But the thing that made Scrooge happiest of all... was that his life lay before him and it could be changed.
Scrooge: Oh. Heaven and the Christmas time be praised for this day. I say it on my knees. Jacob Marley. On my knees. Oh. They're not torn down. They're here. And I'm here. More is the miracle. I don't know what to do. I-I'm as light as a feather. I'm as happy as an angel. I'm... I'm as merry as a schoolboy.
You there. Boy.
Boy: What. Me? Uh. That is. What. Me. Sir?
Scrooge: What's today?
Boy: Pardon?
Scrooge: What's today. My fine fellow?
Boy: Today? Well. Today is Christmas Day.
Scrooge: It's Christmas Day? I haven't missed it. The spirits did it all in one night. They can do anything they like. Of course they can.

3. Ordinary ghosts 2: Violet Hunt

> "I do believe," said the baby farmer, nudging the
> smart woman, "that we shall find he's the man
> who killed his sweetheart and then carefully tied
> her poor insides all into true lover's knots with
> sky-blue ribbon. Artist, indeed! They're quite
> common colours — blue and red ———"
> Violet Hunt, *The Coach*

I'm unsure why I decided on ghosts as a subject, but soon
into my poking around the subject I stumbled onto the
writing of Violet Hunt, specifically the collection *Tales of
the Uneasy*. *Tales of the Uneasy*'s nine stories are not all
ghost stories though some most certainly are. The
supernatural is not a consistent, dependable character
whose effects can be depended on from tale to tale. Yet
each story shares a concern about the border between life
and death, with characters trapped on one side or the
other of this wall, and a few times astride it with a foot in
each state.

A prolific writer (seventeen novels, memoirs, a biography,
extensive diaries), Hunt "liked to think of herself as a
''female rake' who 'snubbed eligibles on principle' and
preferred married men because 'no one could imagine
that I wanted to catch them.'"[29] An active feminist, each

---

[29] Cribbed from a review of a book about Hunt's diaries:
Hodgson, Moira. "A Female Rake." *The New York Times*,
October 21, 1990. Hunt's biography is terribly interesting; for
instance she held literary salons at her home with guests

story in *Tales of the Uneasy* gives its female characters prominence. However (seemingly) in control of their destinies each of these women is Hunt places them at the whims of outside forces both cultural and supernatural, subject to various systems they've no suffrage under (the right to vote in the US still a decade away when *Tales of the Uneasy* was published). At one point in this project I planned on focusing on each of these stories one by one as the basis for the whole text instead of the jumble I've decided on. Eventually that structure may return should I compile these already too-long bits into an even longer whole; for now I'll barrel forward.[30]

---

such as (from her Wiki) Rebecca West, Ezra Pound, Joseph Conrad, Wyndham Lewis, D. H. Lawrence, and Henry James.

[30] Though Sir Arthur Conan Doyle's *The Adventure of the Copper Beeches*'s plot hinges more on a Hitchcockian double, the female protagonist is stand-in for Violet Hunt, a 'Violet Hunter'. It is a tale boiling over with gothic horror staples — a child that is cruel to animals, a frightening demon dog (reminiscent of Doyle's own beasts in *The Hound of the Baskervilles*), a mysterious secret wing of an old mansion. Doyle and Hunt ran in similar circles and were no doubt aware of each other's practices.

In a further connection, the character Violet Hunter recurs in *Sherlock Holmes's War of the Worlds*, an unofficial sequel to *The War of the Worlds*, a strange pastiche/crossover tale by Manly Wade Wellman. In it, Hunter is said to be the wife of the first mate on 'Thunder Child,' a ship that appears in H. G. Wells' *The War of the Worlds.* Wells is one of many authors to whom Hunt's was intimately connected. This is all anecdote — the connection I've made is as much an accident as anything else — a search for 'Violet Hunt' dragging up the character 'Violet Hunter', opening up a worm hole that thankfully I reached the other side of relatively

More often than not, it is as the result of specific, narrative trauma or sacrifice that one hovers, if only briefly (as many times these ghost are merely in transition between states), in a ghostly realm. In Hunt's *The Coach* we have peculiar example of these exemplary cases intertwined with the ordinary dead. After a painfully well-drawn picture of a scene and a road cutting through it ("... viscous with clay here, shining with quartz there, uncompromising, exact, like the lists of old, dressed for a tourney"), we greet a well-dressed man standing, waiting.[31] Eventually his transport arrives, a spectral carriage containing a group of individuals we are then introduced to. They are all ghosts, the man included, being ferried from one place to another.

> I must say I consider this particular system of soul transference that we have to submit to, very unsettling and productive of restlessness amongst us — a mere survival and tiresome superstition, to my mind. It has one merit; one sees something of the under world, traveling about as we do.[32]

But the underworld here is mapped on the land of the living. The group discuss their vices, how they met their

---

unscathed. Maybe the point I'm trying to make is — please name a character Aaron Harbour*sen* or something similar in your next book; spend a few lines describing his remarkable poise.

[31] Hunt, Violet. "The Carriage." In *Tales of the Uneasy*. Ashcroft, B.C.: Ash-Tree, 2004.

[32] Ibid.

individual demises. These are ordinary people in a sense, but, whether or not it is a coincidence or specific to this particular coach, each met a very violent end — a few at the hands of the state. Someone murdered and by happenstance his murderer, a woman who is a 'baby farmer' — a killer of unwanted newborns (darkly, via pure neglect) – they all have generally come to terms with their station in (after)life.[33]

On the road they see in the distance a coach of the living. Their path is unwavering; thought at least mostly invisible to the individuals traveling towards them, the spectral travelers threaten to frighten the approaching coach's horses:

> 'Orses can't abide the sight of us, mostly, no more than they could those nasty motors when they first came in. And we're worst than motors — they seem to smell us out at once for what we are![34]

There is nothing to be done — the horses are startled to calamitous effect:

---

[33] The baby farmer is maligned by her fellow travelers: "Funny, though, how seriously you all take it, even here! The feeling against my profession seems absurdly strong below as above. [...] But those shivering, shrinking women that came to me, some of them hardly out of their teens, some of them so delicate they had no right to have a baby at all! [...] But Lord! – Society, to cry shame on me for it! They might as well hang any other useful public servant, like dustmen, rat-catchers, and such-like ridders of pests."
[34] Ibid.

> I shouldn't be surprised if those two nice girls
> didn't join us at the next stage. If they do, we'll
> make them tell us how they felt, when they first
> saw the coachful of ghosts coming down on
> them. They're certainly dead, for they were both
> pitched into the ditch with the cart and horse on
> top of them.[35]

Fated due this unknown interaction between the under- and over-worlds, these two unknown women meet their fate. These two victims die seemingly randomly, lacking the narrative of the ghost coach's passengers; this is important as we aren't to take the cast of characters as indicative of some special set. These are simply some people experiencing a peculiar purgatory, a liminal passage to which all are subject.

There is a strange comfort to the resignation of all in this story, no grudges, no expressed desire to return haunt them. Of the passengers, the two (relatively) innocents highlight this. One, an older lady whose extravagant gambling lifestyle led a pair of individuals to murder and rob her is terribly understanding, knows she took her liberty too far. The other, the murdered gentleman, despite being of some wealth, was growing weary of life — his only regret that his executioner made out with so

---

[35] Ibid.

little money as he carried little cash on his person. He describes his murder as "[...] a murder most *apropos*."[36]

Though their destination is unknown, no one is fretting their fate. The ghosts in the dream of Prokhorov might take slight issue with the individual who interred them, but they've only been stirred by his request's insensitivity to their plight; otherwise remaining beneath the soil gently rotting away.

---

[36] Ibid. Continued: "I've often longed to get the ear of the jury who tried a man for relieving me of my light purse and intolerably heavy life, and tell them my own proper feelings. [...] I got my desire – kind, speedy, merciful, violent death."

4. Random dying patterns

In the *Mystery Science Theatre 3000* send up of the 1957
Roger Corman western *Gunslinger*, (anti)hero Cain
repeats the well worn dictum

Only the good die young...

to which co-host Tom Servo adds:

*...most of us are morally ambiguous — which explains our
random dying patterns.*

<u>5.</u>

So many memories represent a betrayal by their mere retention, existence.

When out with one's girlfriend in the present one might encounter the past. You were there before with some other girl, it was a pleasant day, you had the hamburger and fries and she her own sandwich I think. You talked about sex, an impending jaunt out of town, you or she pointed out a man alone in Rodney Dangerfield-esque golf attire, you pointed out another girl, peculiar, attractive – neither you or your company are all together sure why she warranted pointing out and this was awkward but not the first time you've been caught with a wandering gaze. You can remember that second girl fairly clearly even years later, what she was wearing, some vague sense of how her mannerisms made her so damn striking as to elude the internal gatekeeper charged with keeping such things unspoken. The only real choice in such situations is to say nothing but somehow this small decency was too much to ask.

In a cartoon, a character might stare off into space at which point a flashback, daydream or some product of their imagination plays. A small movie in their mind reels off... it can go on quite a while, indifferent to the exterior world's sense of time. Something eventually pulls them back into the present; their interlocutor has continued to talk while they didn't listen and perhaps has been saying the character's name, shaking them by the shoulder etc., asking them what's wrong and or accusing them of not listening. Anyway, as rude or socially awkward as these moments come off (usually in a humorous way), it is key that the dreamer never complete relay what has drawn them away from the present.

Likewise one's recollection: to start to tell such a nearly uneventful tale one would come upon two equally uncomfortable endgames.

One – you finish what you've started about this the other-other woman, the striking one never meant – but why would the present company want to know of this paragon, merely glanced at yet deeply emblazoned into memory suggest a path untraveled, regret, dissatisfaction with the current state of affairs.

Two – you could start to tell your story and stop short of the other-other woman. In this case, you've taken it upon yourself to tell a terribly mundane memory involving someone else – you and an ex girlfriend ate food at this place one time. Why would you bring this up? Were you thinking about her, even as the two of us sat knees-touching, reviewing the menu? There are likely more than two paths here – typing this I think of another: elaborate on the flashback conceiving of an another-other-other woman (or man) having a heated, memorable (imagined from scratch? Based on unrelated other memories) argument with the barely-glanced-at person.

A lie tacked on to a mistake; should this exchange come up again it will be elaborated upon, fleshed ever more real. Did you step in to break up this feud? Who of the two – one real and one imagined – is the good guy in the story? There exist a class of ghosts giving gauzy life to those people invented of whole cloth for the sake of obfuscation, distraction, deceit.

6. The Memoir

> Did women in Society ever "speak" to other women,
> when a man dear to them both was concerned?
> - Violet Hunt, *The Memoir*

Clarice Lispector's *Near to the Wild Heart* focuses mostly
on a single, intense character named Joana, specifically on
her relationship to a formerly engaged couple Otavio and
Lídia. Having left his fiancé, Otavio continues seeing
Lídia, who gets pregnant. Lídia, a relatively regular
woman and obtuse Joana, all severe introspection set up a
meeting which fails to resolve their conflict over the man.
As soon as it begins its gears lock, progress ceases:

> "Well," her own tone of voice woke her up
> unpleasantly. "I believe the interview is over."

> Lídia was taken aback. But how? If they hadn't said
> anything! She was particularly put off by the idea of
> something unfinished:

> "We haven't said anything yet... And we need to
> talk..."

> Joana smiled. In this smile she began to act, not with
> force – weariness – but how exactly would I impress
> her. What nonsense am I thinking after all?

> "Don't you feel," said Joana, "that we've gotten away
> from the reason that brought us together? If we

talked about it, now at least, tit would be without interest or passion... Let's leave it all for another day"[37]

Having confronted each other, the long built up energy between the two women is diffused by having met the challenge of meeting face to face. When Joana refers to 'the reason that brought us together' she means that energy, that jealous distemper as an abstract force. Any simple tit-for-tat would do an injustice to that force, render it mundane. *Near to the Wild Heart* elucidates those feelings, those moments of doubt about the continuity of any common spirit across mankind, of the continuity of moments.[38] This discontinuity finds itself highlighted in moments when the practical aspects of individual relationships crash against the difficult to elucidate interior worlds which become ever more disjointed from the every day where love is concerned.

Violet Hunt's *The Memoir* presents a similar dilemma. In it two women, a wife and a mistress speak to one another,

---

[37] Lispector, Clarice. *Near to the wild heart.* London: Penguin Classics, 2014.

[38] From Kafka's diaries, dated January 16, 1922

The clocks are not in unison; the inner one runs crazily on at a devilish or demonic or in any case inhuman pace, the outer one limps along at its usual speed. What else can happen but that the worlds split apart, and they do split apart, or at least clash in a fearful manner.

each so certain of having an aloof, adventurous, flighty man's heart to themselves regardless of his dalliances.

Lady Greenwell wanted nothing more than to tell the young widow Cynthia "Just you let my man alone!"[39]

They manage to get some time alone and they discuss the matter awkwardly – the social norms which bind their mannerisms make it a painful exchange. Lady Greenwall knows she should say something to Cynthia Chenies to dissuade her from being so terribly close to her husband, but how to do so in an honorable, fashionable, classy way stymies her. Cynthia agrees with her doubt as to the potential of their dialogue:

> "I am truly sorry, but, indeed, dear, this sort of carriage lecture never does any good. You can't have straight talk to women. No woman can employ another woman to help keep her husband for her – it really isn't done."

> "Keep my husband! But have I not been telling you, Cynthia, all this time, that if I thought for one moment that my husband had been unfaithful to me in word, or thought, or deed [...]

> "Then it makes it quite simple – go on believing in him."[40]

[39] Hunt, Violet. *Tales of the uneasy*. Ashcroft, B.C.: Ash-Tree, 2004.
[40] Ibid.

They take leave of each other, going so far as to give each other a friendly kiss goodbye.

> "[...] You know I am really fond of you, Cynthia, but you seem to have beaten me."

> "Oh, no!" asservated Mrs. Chenies, "only convinced you that these sort of things can't be done."[41]

What a ghost says is true – though whose truth is never so certain. The tale rushes forward a year; Mr. Greenwell has died off on some adventure; Lady Greenwell calls Cynthia to see her.

> "And Hilary said – dear thing! – when he left me to go on that wretched expedition that killed him, that I was to be as nice to you as I could."

But rather than meeting simply to commiserate over their mutual love's death – awkward as that would be – Lady Greenwell has in her possession Hilary Greenwell's memoir. She has asked for Cynthia to be present to help edit the document to be published, but as importantly to bear witness to the text's reinforcement of her position that his love for her was unflappable, with side pieces like Cynthia almost unremarked upon in his record.

---

[41] Ibid.

"It is really rather too intimate!" Lady Greenwall blurted out. "Listen to this – *'Darling, my darling'* I can scarcely bear to read it. *'All night I lie and toss on my uncomfortable rugs and think – think of you darling, and your soft breast!'*"

"You might put 'cheek' there, instead of 'breast,' if you liked?" interposed the co-editress hastily.

The document continues in that vein, espousing the virtues of his wife, making the mistress increasingly distraught.

Give me some hot water to drink," gasped Mrs. Chenies. "Is — this your revenge, Mabel?"
"Dear Cynthia, aren't you well? You do use such odd stagey words. Revenge! I am your friend and always will be. My husband wanted us to be friends."[42]

The dead-man' missives hang between two possible truths, his own (whether true or fabricated/augmented as to suit his audience's desire), as likely, those of Lady Greenwall who may have as easily forged the papers to hurt her gentleman's suitor. Though this latter possibility is left unspoken, a ghost necessarily imbues the world with two truths: the manifestation of the guilt and desires of the dead, and those of the living.

---

[42] Ibid.

When a ghost accuses the living of a sin, is the subconscious of ghost's seer conjuring the spirit to make present their interior shame? Or, in a special case of empathy, does the cessation of breath of person allow another to collapse the dead's life into a message revealing a previously unknown truth?

7. No gravity; then gravity twice

a.

As a child I would be left for a time at the entrance of the grocery store (at my request). I liked the toy section of certain stores, and I've always been into the large magazine sections which used to be commonplace, but these were outweighed by the draw of the one or two video games near the door and the candy machines. And the strange joy of stepping on the rubber mat actuator of the automatic doors, an invention made common long before my time yet somehow still impressive to the young me.[43] But quite often, sneakers pressed against mat, the door would refuse to slide open. I could imagine scenarios in dreams where this would occur and I'd be unable to exit whatever grave danger stalked me through the aisles. Surely it failed to open because I was tall but frail and some minimum threshold whereby the door sensed the need to move was close enough to my weight as to ignore it, but I couldn't escape the impression I maybe didn't exist, I maybe was a ghost.[44]

---

[43] Googling "what year did automatic doors" (not the best phrasing but I'm looking at it, and it is what I used...) returns a pre-response answer of "'From When the Sleeper Wakes', by H.G. Wells. The first automatic sliding doors for use by people were invented in 1954 by Lew Hewitt and Dee Horton; the first one was installed in 1960. It made use of a mat actuator." It was with a big smile that I found the lead character on the third season of the television show Fargo suffering with the same malady.

[44] I think I saw this after this sensation making it that much more eerie, but in a fondly remembered episode of *The Simpsons*, "Bart Sells His Soul", (which he doesn't believe

b.

On the walk to work, on a roughly manicured berm between community college and street, there are some trees pruned all the way back to the start in some sense from whose calloused and swollen post-main-trunk-split grow its branches (all winter-bare) interspersed with low bushes whose foliage is gone leaving a fruitless bramble. In the latter are worn the fallen, well-browned leaves of the former. They've fallen and been either pressed into the void left by lost leaves in between twigs or have been speared improbably by the branch ends. A creature, (*playing*) dead, wearing the shed skin of another.

c.

A strange hobby: a friend and I would look for hard to reach outdoorsy places in San Francisco. He'd bring an old top-loading tape deck and some reggae mixes, I'd bring a vague plan. One especially nice day we clamored around the hills and cliffs between China Beach and the Sutro Baths. There are several not-too-hard to climb down to beaches and small caves to explore, along with strange graffiti spots, wonderful small trees, relative seclusion. The coast is steep and juts out here and there; at low tide you can more or less scramble over rocks or

---

exists) to a more than happy to deal Milhouse. The family pets respond coldly to him, an automatic door fails to open for him; Bart becomes increasingly frightened and tries to get back his 'soul', now owned by Comic Store Guy. It is a weird premise — the writers of the episode clearly are advocating for the real existence of a soul.

wade around them to access another stretch of sand, another cavelet. But from above, on the path atop the cliff face, one can see even more of these beautiful alcoves far below, seemingly a quick (if sketchy) jaunt down. But scale and distance can be deceiving.

I thought I spotted a way down to a particularly idyllic spot. As the hill descended there were intermittent pine trees of various sizes and gnarled roots kicking up here and there through a bed of dried needles; I imagined that with some ease I could, on my back, scuttle down, sliding almost, from point-to-point most of the way down. My friend was unimpressed with my plan but willing to follow. The first little bit went smooth, but it got steeper and steeper and my grip upon the earth less certain. *Slip* — then catch my footing on a small outcropping. *Slip* — ever less certain but again my foot digs in, this time on the root of a cyprus tree. The foliage is thinning now; I've not traveled more than a dozen yards but it already feels perilously far to climb back up and a way down has not made itself apparent. And what's more, how far exactly we are from the beach below is in question. From the path I could see the waves crashing but from where I am now all I see is the ocean. Another few feet crawled and then — *slip* — the big slip, I've no control now and am accelerating fast, sliding on my back, falling, my glasses tumble off, I'm falling, falling, what was only a ridge before now appears as a cliff.

Sliding, falling fast, now certain I'll die should I go over the edge (I would have). At the last possible moment I reach out and grab the frail trunk of a few-feet-high tree which at this point is hardly three inches round and *over* —

I can remember clear as day what was going on in my mind as I fell. Not memories, regrets, gods, loved ones, family. Simply this phrase, in my voice, deeper and more certain than it was at that age, saying '*DON'T DIE.*'

I'm over the edge, hanging on by only the tree, very much like in a movie. I look down — it is twenty or thirty feet straight down to some large boulders. I quickly, somehow, charged by adrenaline to overcome my intense weakness and lack of upper body strength, pull myself up and back onto the ledge. My friend is halfway down yelling for me; I yell back that I'm okay. On my belly I start to crawl back up, slowly, loosing my grip a bit now and then on the slippery pine needle slope. On the way up I find my glasses, just laying there as if on a bedside table. Eventually I get far enough my friend can help me the rest of the way; we clamber up; we're back on the path. My clothes are filthy, torn all over. I'm hurt and bleeding, but we're kinda laughing?

We cackled hard about it. Painful, deep, unstoppable laughter, as hard as I've ever laughed in my life. All the while I was bleeding through my shredded t-shirt; no deep wounds but enough to discourage such a fall again; in the back of my mind I tried to plot my explanation to my girlfriend of my sorry state. Dirty, bloody, laughing.

_D._

1.

> "Very well; poke the fire into a blaze – so ; and now,
> if you are all ready, I will begin, and remember, what
> I am going to tell you is really and literally true. It
> happened to – myself; and if it is not 'horrible'
> enough, I can't help it."
> -The Countess of Muenster, *Mauvais Quart
> D'heure*[45]

Ghost stories are always presented as "really and literally
true." This gesture persists in contemporary ghost/horror
cinema which more often than not elucidates in previews
and in text at the beginning of the film that it is 'based on
true events'. Herein a surprising amount has been 'based
on true events'. I would not have guessed this direction
when I began this project, thinking this would proceed in
a research-write direction like the last long thing I made.
Instead, a long period of research-write was followed by a
write-write period in which research took a back seat to
memoir-ish rambling.

---

[45] A 'mauvais quart d'heure' is a French phrase used as a
colloquialism for a brief unpleasant period, from the
French meaning literally a 'bad quarter of an hour'. Long
out of fashion (if it ever was in use in the US); it seems an
idea worthy of being given a word(s), idiom etc. as I don't
think we've anything in circulation which covers this
territory

The question became (answered obviously, judging by this object in your hands) whether or not to call any version of this finished. Whether to allow whatever I write to glom on to the mass of it and find itself in print or to grant the original bits finality, forcing what follows to find their own outlet physical or otherwise.

A plan – stay loose, drag out the conclusion a bit but let it go when it goes.

2.

> The life had probably not been of the most vivid
> order: for long periods, no doubt, it had fallen as
> noiselessly into the past as the quiet drizzle of
> autumn fell, hour after hour, into the green fish-
> pond between the yews; but these back-waters of
> existence sometimes breed, in their sluggish depths,
> strange acuities of emotion, and Mary Boyne had
> felt from the first the occasional brush of an intenser
> memory.
> -Edith Wharton, *Afterwards*

Slowing to a crawl. I've no interest in fabricating yet am
guilty of so much omission – are lies the moral equivalent
of redactions? Unsure.

What does it look like when I'm overextended, one or
more too many responsibilities (all of my own making)
flooding the hours of the day and the levee is breached?

3. The biographic & an introduction to Lafcadio Hearn

> Writing isn't an easy taskmaster. Sentences left
> unfinished never continue as well as they had
> begun. New ideas bend the main arch of the text,
> and it never again sits perfectly true.
> — Magda Szabó, *The Door*

I don't care about your ghost story, your ghostly
experience. Not really. In the same way I'm disinterested
in your personal moment with god(s), this or that prayer
that was answered, your miracles et al. But let's read your
holy books together, let me see the story you made up.
Truth, as a fiction through exclusion, with or without the
imposition of my own desires and points of reference
filling in the blanks, is a bit boring, tells me less about the
world than your story, than a legend told seventh-hand.

Easy enough to say. And yet this text is peppered with my
own biographical tidbits, many mostly true. Hypocrisy,
sure. The teller assumes the relevance of their anecdotes
while being barely able to stifle a yawn when subjected to
another's, sometimes. I feel likewise about the lives of
artists — biography is so often used to buttress a practice
which may, given room to breath, say more without it.
And yet...
Born in 1850 in Greece, Lafcadio Hearn had a very
complicated childhood. Moving around a bunch, he
settled with his great aunt in Ireland and Wales at the age
of seven, though both his parents were still alive. At
sixteen he injured (and eventually went blind in) one of

his eyes. A few years later the young and restless but intelligent boy, who had moved to Cincinnati, was given five dollars and essentially abandoned. Eventually, he would start writing for a newspaper until his writings for a satirical magazine and his vocally anti-religious views so angered business and clergy that they used his (then illegal) marriage to a black woman the pretense to have him fired. Always outside, unrooted, Hearn was an adventurous reporter and chronicler of the world, writing about local black culture while in Ohio, moving to New Orleans and getting equally deep into that culture, then spending a pair of years in the West Indies where he chronicled his time there along with penning *Youma, The Story of a West-Indian Slave.*

He later settled in Japan and it was here he found a true calling of sorts. Many a white American or European has been entranced by all things "Oriental" — so strange are the customs and culture of Asian cultures to a newcomer — and to be sure it would be an oversight not to note in his writings in Japan and elsewhere a strong element of exoticism and Orientalism. But I think always outside, always searching, Hearn was uniquely equipped for his research. All was other to him whether immersed in the Midwest, Southern Creole black culture, or in Japan.

He went on to write over fifteen books about Asian culture, especially focusing on folklore and the supernatural in works such as *Some Chinese Ghosts, In Ghostly Japan*, and most famously *Kwaidan: Stories and Studies of Strange Things.* To quote Hearn:

I sought especially for weird beauty; and I could not forget this striking observation in Sir Walter Scott's *Essay on Imitations of the Ancient Ballad*: "The supernatural, though appealing to certain powerful emotions very widely and deeply sown amongst the human race, is, nevertheless, a spring which is peculiarly apt to lose its elasticity by being too much pressed upon."[46]

---

[46] See the 1964 Masaki Kobayashi film *Kwaidan* for a great dramatization of some of these stories. It speaks to the extent to which Hearn managed to capture his subject that a Japanese filmmaker of Kobayashi's strength would choose his works as the basis for his production.

4. Three ambiguities in Lafcadio Hearn's Kwaidan[47]

a.

In *A Dead Secret*, a dead woman named O-Sono reappears in ghostly form and a priest is called to root out the purpose of the spectre's distemper. The ghost hovers around a chest holding the deceased's personal belongings.

> He searched the chest from top to bottom. In the last drawer he found — a letter. "Is this the thing that troubles you?" O-Sono's gaze fixed upon the letter.
>
> "Shall I burn it for you?" O-Sono then bowed before him.
> He promised her that he would burn it that very morning. "No one shall read it, except myself."
>
> The figure then smiled and vanished.[48]

He finds that she has kept a love letter from an infatuation she had while in school prior to meeting her

---

[47] Moments when the texts remain incomplete or certain omissions are made. Hearn maintains a fealty to the source, not filling in blanks where they exist, maintaining ambiguities. His light hand, not over-Westernizing the works, is what makes these tales retain a wonder not simply couched in either the author's pen or exoticism.

[48] All the quotes in this section are drawn from the stories mentioned therein in Hearn, Lafcadio. *Kwaidan*. Boston: Houghton Mifflin Co., 1923.

husband. But the letter's details are omitted from the text. The text ends without the narrator or priest revealing the contents of the letter; her secret dies with the priest. This is a story of an erasure: we know the act is performed but what was erased is left unspoken in keeping with the ghost's desire. We are adjoined to the world of the tale by our lack, by what we don't know, what O-Sono felt it best no one ever know.

It is not a given that a truth is readable; that there remains some record deducible from forensics, the written record, oral history et al. Rather, the bulk of what happens is obliterated – and even should there be evidence enough to construe a secret it will remain un-unearthed (earthed?) as there remains the requisite for someone to desire to know.

The contemporary library is full of people, there to bask in its physical resources (climate control, seating, restrooms etc.) and to make use of the internet there. A subsection of patrons really do research a specific topic using the mass of books contained within; but this minority leaves the bulk of the building's holdings unleafed through. Therein is the difference between the knowable and the never-to-be-known. But to recognize the general obscurity of a record isn't to be completely comforted at its safety.

The fealty of this tale to the desire of the ghost beyond a general hint at some impropriety however vague – the mere admittance of a former love whether acted upon or not being enough to warrant the spirit's affliction – plays with our entitlement as readers to know all, an expectation that a story eventually provide us secrets unknowable in the non-fictionalized relationships we hold.

b.

In *Of a Mirror and a Bell*, after an introduction to concept of *nazoraeru*, a kind of virtue-based exchange of value:

> The word itself cannot be adequately rendered by any English word; for it is used in relation to many kinds of mimetic magic, as well as in relation to the performance of many religious acts of faith. Common meanings of nazoraeru, according to dictionaries, are "to imitate," "to compare," "to liken;" but the esoteric meaning is to substitute, in imagination, one object or action for another, so as to bring about some magical or miraculous result.

For example — you cannot afford to build a Buddhist temple; but you can easily lay a pebble before the image of the Buddha with the same pious feeling that would prompt you to build a temple if you were rich enough to build one. The merit of so offering the pebble becomes equal, or almost equal, to the merit of erecting a temple...

Artist Felix Gonzalez-Torres's practice gave surprising physicality to the most ethereal of legends. Kafka's description of a discrepancy between interior and external clocks is brought to life by a pair of 'identical' clocks whose times slowly drift from their initial in tune state; stand ins for a couple once tightly moored in love are slowly untied and though unpropelled, nevertheless grow apart. A pile of candy is indifferently (as far as the artist is concerned) arranged the weight of the artist's dead lover, and the audience is strangely emboldened to not only touch the work but to take of it, to pick up a piece of candy, unwrap and eat it. The candies are eventually replaced – the stack is eternal, and yet somehow ever more diffuse. Here both the body of Christ as sacrament and one of Christ's miracles by which a loaf of bread and glass of wine is enough to feed a multitude are replicated, and the repetition of a loved one's wasting at the hands of AIDS is reperformed, never forgotten.

Eternity, something seemingly intransigent, is intermixed with a strange element of contingency. Death is transgressed as a human retains a permanent echo in the form of an object... Gonzalez-Torres's works are infinitely reiterable, one simply needs to go to the store and buy some more candy, resync the clocks etc. They deny ever being definitive, having a finished, permanent, consistent state.

Hearn's piece begins with a tale ending in a tragic, angry suicide that becomes legendary. A woman who donated her mirror to a great bell's creation did so without all of her heart and it wouldn't melt in the foundry, causing her great shame. As she died, she declared "to the person who breaks that bell by ringing it, great wealth will be given by the ghost of me." People traveled from far and wide and did their best to break the thing, to the point that the priest had the thing taken down and rolled into a swamp.

The legend continued despite the bell's disappearance. An individual in great need destroyed a brass basin, a convenient effigy which mentally representing the bell, and through *nazoraeru* the ghostly promised good fortune came. Others hearing this story did their best to repeat the process. A farmer who had fallen upon bad times (of his own making) "made for himself, out of the mud in his garden, a clay-model of the Mugen-Kane; and he beat the clay-bell, and broke it, — crying out the while for great wealth." A spirit appeared to the man, presenting him with a jar: "I have come to answer your fervent prayer as it deserves to be answered."

> Into his house the happy man rushed, to tell his wife the good news. He set down in front of her the covered jar, — which was heavy, — and they opened it together. And they found that it was filled, up to the very brim, with...
> But no! — I really cannot tell you with what it was filled.

We are left here — the story leaves the farmer's fate unknown. The miraculous is fickle, furtive; we doubt whether the man is deserving of good fortune but whether the jar contains a second chance for the man or comeuppance (is empty, has something terrifying or worthless within) is left unspoken.

c.

Here and there the tales Hearn chooses to relay have a real terror streak to them, with imagery not out of place in a horror film. The persistence of what frightens across such distances in time and culture is impressive — there are some universally terrifying images and circumstances.

Mujina is a brief tale. There is a small region of wild which is avoided, travelers going well out of their way to avoid a mujina, a kind of shapeshifter/animal spirit demon. Shared is a man's tale of his encounter with the spirit. Hearing a woman in trouble, he stopped to ask her what was the matter.[49] Her face is hidden behind hair and the sleeves of her garment but eventually she

> turned around, and dropped her sleeve, and stroked her face with her hand; — and the man saw that she had no eyes or nose or mouth, — and he screamed and ran away.

The man runs through the dark, dark night, spotting a lantern in the distance, that of an itinerant soba-seller. The soba-man can tell the man is frightened and asks him what is the matter, had anybody hurt him? Had he been robbed?

---

[49] Here the narrator notes: "He really meant what he said; for he was a very kind man." This serves to allay any implication that what follows is deserved and not what it is — a whim of the unknowable.

"Not robbers, — not robbers," gasped the terrified man... "I saw... I saw a woman — by the moat; — and she showed me... Ah! I cannot tell you what she showed me!"...

"He! Was it anything like THIS that she showed you?" cried the soba-man, stroking his own face — which therewith became like unto an Egg... And, simultaneously, the light went out.

5. a quote submitted without comment, to be thought about in a future version

Let me illustrate what I mean from an experiment which Paracelsus describes as not difficult, and which the author of the *Curiosities of Literature* cites as credible: A flower perishes; you burn it. Whatever were the elements of that flower while it lived are gone, dispersed, you know not whither; you can never discover nor recollect them. But you can, by chemistry, out of the burnt dust of that flower, raise a spectrum of the flower, just as it seemed in life. It may be the same with the human being. The soul has as much escaped you as the essence or elements of the flower. Still you may make a spectrum of it. And this phantom, though in the popular superstition it is held to be the soul of the departed, must not be confounded with the true soul; it is but the eidolon of the dead form.[50]

---

[50] Lytton, Edward Bulwer Lytton. *The haunted and the haunters, or, The house and the brain*. Chicago: Rajput Press, 1911.An eidolon: a phantom, a shade/shadow, an unsubstantial image, often an ideal but definitely not the thing itself.

6. Not quite ghosts, yet...

This thing became as much about ghost stories-proper as it did about analogs, strange exceptions to the natural order lurking in plain sight all around. This project, or phase of this project anyway, is adrift. I'd write a bit about Julien Gracq's *Au château d'Argol*, a ghost-less tale which couches a psychological drama between three people told completely without dialogue in a wash of gothic horror staples. I'd dig deeper into *Uneasy Tales*.

And then what started simply enough began to drown in remembrances, anecdotes, asides. Once completed the original bones of the thing will jut out like ruins in a jungle or fossils in an otherwise homogenous strata of stone.

In Magda Szabó's *The Door*, a writer and her husband are afforded the care of a powerful spectre of a woman in a small Hungarian town. Terribly secretive, meting out attention and personal narrative according to her intense sense of privacy and justice, she chooses to work for the couple, and in various capacities most of the townsfolk, versus the other way around.

The main character is managing to be fairly successful despite the doubt of one's own abilities, which seems more the norm than the exception for most creative types, and despite the recently perilous and still tenuous political situation in Hungary. She's so successful that she is awarded a prestigious award and is asked to be a member of a delegation to an international conference.

Emerence sees right through her, in the fiercest, most biting way. Everything about her is a challenge to the author — morally good while shunning Christianity, absolutely dismissive of cognitive labor, valuing those who sweep above those who read.

Emerence, appearing in their life out of nowhere, with a terribly gothic backstory, is as likely to disappear at any moment. Severe, seemingly invincible, only pride and her own sense of justice might break the woman. Her heavily guarded abode, into which no one is granted admission (fueling neighborhood speculation about what manner of treasures might be hoarded within) is not her own — the property of the building which she manages, shifted to the next manager upon her departure. And her things, spectral treasures, might dissolve along with her.

Guilt, a sense of being unworthy of the privilege afforded one, has conjured Emerence into the narrator's life. She and her husband develop a codependence with this living embodiment of both the haphazard nature of morality and their unfairly unprecarious place in the world.

In this light, even the title, which at first might seem a bit low-hanging metaphoric foothold (for the secretive, the withheld etc.), begins to recall the name of any number of ghost stories; 'The X', for instance, *The Raven*, or Hunt's in *Tales of the Uneasy* (all falling under this rubric *The Telegram, The Coach, The Tiger-Skin*...). In *The Door* a world of rational, educated people who believe in science and religion are parried by something more ancient, someone who denies religion yet remains pious, someone for whom communing with animals is almost the only way to house her dangerously fealtous love.

Forgive this detour towards an over-litigated subject,
somewhat out of place in this project but no more so than
much of what I'm trying to pass off as connected.

What is forever missing is a real understanding of what
happens when you take a photograph and paint it.
Sublimity, beauty, a slight remove from the source, the
ability to furl and unfurl the so-solid surface that is a
photo. Certain things beyond the realm of photography's
ability to capture might be revealed or invented out of
whole cloth. But what if the image is as such that it
demands itself closed to revision (beyond the natural
compression and decompression of digital file circulation
and the myriad printing processes via which it was
distributed in the press)? Drafting the open casket photo
in the service of her aesthetic practice with the purpose
that it need be seen, based on an empathy that she
acknowledges can only ever be partial (what empathy can
ever be said to be close to complete? Watching himself
from within a spectral realm, Scrooge's experiences are
doubled; young twins in matching attire are playing in
the kitchen and one cuts her hand...) Schutz transgresses.
Like calling 'Bloody Mary' or Beetlejuice, it is somewhere
in the excess of repetitions that the image falters. It is one
thing to feel empathy — we watch a film and cry as a
character we've loved (perhaps over many films/ seasons
but maybe for just for the duration of the program) dies.
It is what we do with this feeling that matters. Feeling
another's pain, does reproduction and/or revision grant a

place of distance where at this pain can be considered, or does it pile on, distract, mask.

Mamie Till, presented with the norm — the dressing up through the mortuary arts of a body so as to seem blissful, a pinch away from simply waking up but happier somehow in their repose — chose instead to give the real. A harsh reality; sickening, heartbreaking. Christina Sharpe in an interview on *Hyperallergic* notes:

> So Mamie Till refuses to have those images not be shown. And she says (this isn't a direct quote): *Look at what they did to my son. This is my son. Look at what they did to him.* She insists that the violence that he has been subject to be seen, unobscured. It seems to me that what Dana Schutz has done is to take that unobscured violence and make it abstract. Mamie Till wanted to make violence real. And that thing — white supremacy, violent abduction, murder — that Mamie Till wanted to make absolutely clear is abstracted in Schutz's work, and in her defense of the work.[51]

The act perpetrated on this young man resulted in a body caught between two identities — the young man, his past

---

[51] Mitter, Siddhartha. ""What Does It Mean to Be Black and Look at This?" A Scholar Reflects on the Dana Schutz Controversy." *Hyperallergic*. March 25, 2017. Accessed March 25, 2017. http://hyperallergic.com/368012/what-does-it-mean-to-be-black-and-look-at-this-a-scholar-reflects-on-the-dana-schutz-controversy/.

and potential; and bare violence. "Look what they've done to *my son*," yes, but also "*look what they do!*" – white supremacist violence, the holding of black life as lacking in value, disposable. What sort of spirit is conjured by Schutz's work? The kind which burdens the living with its excess of suffering, a reminder, a remnant? *You will never be forgiven for what you've done, you will never be allowed to move on, to forget.* Or one of anguish, never allowed to rest, misused, held in a loop, suffering violence eternally like Prometheus's liver?

An image can harm — they do so less frequently perhaps than words or actions but they may harm nonetheless. Reproduced in Schutz's painting is not the person but the violence; the work's ornament sits in direct opposition to the deceased mother's wishes, represents a second defacement, however well-intentioned its fabrication may have been.[52]

---

[52] This is where I depart from Coco Fusco's declaration that "The most perplexing criticism that's been bandied about regarding Schutz's painting, both on social media and in discussions I've had, is that some great harm has been inflicted by the act of abstraction, as if the only 'responsible' treatment of racial trauma is mimetic realism." Rather, there is nothing perplexing about this criticism: it is abstraction, a "painted face" as expected for the dead as something directly in opposition to the victim's mother's simple request (that Till be seen as is) which stings most. Fusco's text (as with everything she writes) is definitely worth digging through: Fusco, Coco. "Censorship, Not the Painting, Must Go: On Dana Schutz's Image of Emmett Till." *Hyperallergic*. March 27, 2017. Accessed March 28, 2017.
https://hyperallergic.com/368290/censorship-not-the-painting-must-go-on-dana-schutzs-image-of-emmett-till/.

E.

1. Becoming

An undefining; not quite an inversion. Edges are blurred,
normal opacity is shed, perhaps the mostly dead-matte
and light-absorptive finish of the human form is
augmented by an ethereal glow and a semi-opacity. The
normal friction at the point of encounter between body
and world slips. Walls may still function as barriers to
vision but their capacity to hold you in is lost.

What are your motivations in this strange new state?
Why not a rebirth? Why be confined to the past-you,
dead and buried on the other side?

-

Fragments stumbled upon in my notes that I can't quite
settle on have being written by me or found in someone
else's text (more than likely the later, or a hybrid):

> Sadness as so unbearable in *this world* that this
> world must be defied – it is the only way it is to
> be remained in. The dead must rise in order that
> I can rest and or depart.

Let's affix this to an attributable quote, one from
Dostoevsky's *Crime and Punishment*

> "There are three ways before her," he thought,
> "the canal, the madhouse, or . . . at last to sink

into depravity which obscures the mind and turns the heart to stone."

The last idea was the most revolting, but he was a skeptic, he was young, abstract, and therefore cruel, and so he could not help believing that the last end was the most likely.[53]

---

[53] Dostoyevsky, Fyodor. *Crime and Punishment*. New York: The Modern Library, 1994.

2. Haunted Houses

No human eye can isolate the unhappy coincidence of line and place which suggests evil in the face of a house, and yet somehow a maniac juxtaposition, a badly turned angle, some chance meeting of roof and sky, turned Hill House into a place of despair, more frightening because the face of Hill House seemed awake, with a watchfulness from the blank windows and a touch of glee in the eyebrow of a cornice. Almost any house, caught unexpectedly or at an odd angle, can turn a deeply humorous look on a watching person; even a mischievous little chimney, or a dormer like a dimple, can catch up a beholder with a sense of fellowship; but a house arrogant and hating, never off guard, can only be evil. This house, which seemed somehow to have formed itself, flying together into its own powerful pattern under the hands of its builders, fitting itself into its own construction of lines and angles, reared its great head back against the sky without concession to humanity. It was a house without kindness, never meant to be lived in, not a fit place for people or for love or for hope. Exorcism cannot alter the countenance of a house; Hill House would stay as it was until it was destroyed.[54]

---

[54] Jackson, Shirley. *The masterpieces of Shirley Jackson: The Lottery, The Haunting of Hill House, We Have Always Lived in the Castle*. London: Raven Books, 1996. NOTE: This chapter is half-done, requiring a great deal of work to complete that won't happen prior to an initial print run. Yet there is some useful content within, I hope.

There is a haunted house; for one reason or another (an inheritance, a dare, an investigation) an individual or group of people are drawn to spend time there. Their arrival is auspicious but not over alarming, with only light disturbances the first night. These grow in intensity as the visit wears on, resulting in some calamity or calamities. There are two types of entities to deal with in these narratives – the ghosts of deceased predecessors and the house/structure itself.

Such it seems is the fate of interactions with a haunted house – these narratives are very much about fate. A chain of events is set into motion, or as often a long since begun sequence is adjoined to the destiny of an unsuspecting group or individual, caught in the wheels and dragged forward. In Shirley Jackson's *The Haunting of Hill House* a group is drawn by a doctor interested in the supernatural, a Dr. John Montague, to a haunted house, amongst which is Eleanor – mousy, private, awkward – her running away onto this venture the defining feature in an otherwise uneventful life:

> During the whole underside of her life, ever since her first memory, Eleanor had been waiting for something like Hill House.[55][56]

---

[55] Ibid.

[56] Such people are all around us. At work, a coworker in another part of the office laughs, chuckles? A muffled, Mutley laugh, mostly air; it's hard not to imagine her hand over her mouth. Where do our affectations come from? What of our quirks are shadows cast by events long past? I can

We watch as this temporary community naturally develops a dynamic as all such groups do. Though each, basically unknown to each other at the start, has the opportunity to reinvent themselves in accordance with aspirations and/or desires they all refuse this potential. Eleanor specifically becomes more and more *who she is*:

> what a complete and separate thing I am, she thought, going from my red toes to the top of my head, individually am I, possessed of attributes belonging only to me. I have red shoes, she thought—that goes with being Eleanor; I dislike lobster and sleep on my left side and crack my knuckles when I am nervous and save buttons. I am holding a brandy glass which is mine because I am here and I am using it and I have a place in this

---

imagine this woman as a girl, boisterous, a brash energy, unabashed joy. Kid jokes can be stunners, real works of art. This can be missed in the moment as you, adult, can see they don't get what you consider the fundamentals of a joke to be – they don't understand the form of pun, the function of a certain slant-rhyme of continuity from beginning to end, an upending of logic through the insertion of keen observation, language's lacunae gazed into... Instead nonsense, forbidden words and/or words that are for whatever reason fun to say lead the charge.

A loud, clear laugh, shrill and sharp, flashing across the restaurant or classroom in an unignorable torrent – to her parents, teachers peers: she must be hushed, muted somewhat. Taught to hold it in, to produce a slight, polite affect. But alas, a respectful snicker, a knowing nod is a poor replacement for ebullience – she so prone to delight, pure and electric.

room. I have red shoes and tomorrow I will wake up and I will still be here.[57]

The agenda of the spirits in the house is never made clear nor are their history, there is only an abstract dread which continues to build, growing ever more frightening after an initial thrill at the appearance of the paranormal. Haunted houses may be given specific spirits dwelling within, but regardless the houses themselves are described so as to provide them human or animal-like agency. In Steven King's *The Shining*, The Overlook hotel takes on an ominous character.

> Flakes of snow swirled and danced across the porch. The Overlook faced it as it had for nearly three-quarters of a century, its darkened windows now bearded with snow, indifferent to the fact it was now cut off from the world... Inside its shell the three of them went about their early evening routine, like microbes trapped in the intestine of a monster.[58]

The Overlook is a meta spirit built upon the compounded suffering, death and violence it had encompassed over its lifetime ("Any big hotels have got scandals," he said. "Just like every big hotel has got a ghost."[59])

---

[57] Ibid.
[58] King, Stephen. *The Shining*. New York, NY: Pocket Books, 2002.
[59] Ibid.

Hill House is similarly charged but Jackson eschews this cause and effect rationalization. Upon arriving, Eleanor's foreboding first impression was repulsion:

> She shivered and thought, the words coming freely into her mind, Hill House is vile, it is diseased; get away from here at once.[60]

Each of the visitors has their own experiences with the home but for Eleanor these events are all the more acute; she sees things no one else does as she is somehow especially attune to such things, having had such an experience in childhood.

Dr. Montague's wife arrives at the house along with her male 'companion' and they proceed to take over the show, stereotypical methods of speaking to the undead including *planchette*, a Ouija board like contraption.[61]

---

[60] Jackson, *The Haunting of Hill House*

[61] "We've gotten a good deal of information for you," Mrs. Montague said. "Now. Planchette was quite insistent about a nun. Have you learned anything about a nun, John?"
"In Hill House? Not likely."
"Planchette felt very strongly about a nun, John. Perhaps something of the sort—a dark, vague figure, even—has been seen in the neighborhood? Villagers terrified when staggering home late at night?"
"The figure of a nun is a fairly common—"
"John, if you please. I assume you are suggesting that I am mistaken. Or perhaps it is your intention to point out that planchette may be mistaken? I assure you—and you must believe planchette, even if my word is not good enough for you—that a nun was most specifically suggested."

Seemingly transported from an earlier century, these two characters represent a curious trope of ghost stories beginning with a take down of lesser stories before the main one begins. They are said to be frivolous while the one being presented is more real, or else as in the beginning of Henry James's *The Turn of the Screw*, we join in as another story is being told, only to have one of those in the audience declare that he has his own tale:

> "I quite agree—in regard to Griffin's ghost, or whatever it was—that its appearing first to the little boy, at so tender an age, adds a particular touch. But it's not the first occurrence of its charming kind that I know to have involved a child. If the child gives the effect another turn of the screw, what do you say to TWO children—?"
> "We say, of course," somebody exclaimed, "that they give two turns!"[62]

In *The Haunting of Hill House* the fakery is inserted directly into a scene that we and the other characters believe needs no such trumping up of wisps of the wind, as there is indeed something unwell brewing in the home. Eleanor's transformation and connection to the house becomes increasingly worrisome, preying on her insecurity and

---

[62] James, Henry. *The Turn of the Screw and Other Short Fiction*. New York: Bantam Dell, 2008. In The *Turn of the Screw* it is only after a prolonged pulling of teeth that the eventual narrator gives up his story; similarly the story fights itself with endless innuendo muddying what might otherwise be a better than average story.

I am learning the pathways of the heart, Eleanor
thought quite seriously, and then wondered what
she could have meant by thinking any such thing.[63]

There is a ramping up of paranormal experiences while
simultaneously Eleanor gets more and more lost in
infatuation with her fellow guests. On one frightful
evening she is drawn by the house onto a high window
ledge she has to be gently talked down from. Everyone is
thoroughly uncomfortable after this near death situation;
the story concludes once another turn of the screw is
made.

---

[63] Jackson, *The Haunting of Hill House*

The wind has gone,
The invisible come
Your memories are being run
- Broadcast, 'Echo's Answer'

'There's no such thing as ghosts, not really anyway' but this hardly calms one down, gives one solace – neither death as absolute nor immortality feel good enough. That being a ghost should be such an experience of unease feels proper to the role.

The camera lingered on a man tying his shoes. In red white and blue head-to-toe, surrounded by a sea of green, all in the crowd both present and tele-visual waited patiently. Cuba was playing the Netherlands at baseball, in Japan.

Behind me two young men chatter away about this or that comedy and their own tedious ambition to record their ideas for skits and sketches. Their every word is like nails on a chalkboard – familiar, as I am tedious man and was once a young man but I've the ambition to not be this type of person anymore and they offer an unwelcome reminder of a certain kind of white, privileged, smarter-than-average (but not usefully so) person which holds too firm a grip on the direction of the world despite their unworthiness to helm anything beyond their own drift to anonymity.

I feel no more or less alive thinking heavy thoughts.
You'd be excused while awash in some extreme of
melancholy to feel that you and only you, or at least only
those so far towards an emotional pole are more present,
more alive than that guy at the bar staring at the volume-
less commercials during a basketball game time out, than
the couple splitting a sandwich in relative silence, each
having exhausted the tale of their respective days at work.
You'd be wrong. If anything, the opposite may be true.
Hyper aware of one's inner workings, you are that much
further from the world's relentless mediocrity, inanity.

The wind is near
The invisible hear
Come my thoughts away from fear

Oh, the wind will come
Blow,
Answer...
all these...

echoes

4

One of the keys to my understanding sonically the songs 'Miel' and 'Desafío' off of the incredible 2017 self-titled album by Arca is the Bjork song 'Cocoon' on her 2001 *Vespertine*. On that album Bjork's love is so terribly in full bloom, the fade of the blossom teasingly on the horizon. There is a fragility to it all, a bare sexuality, disconcertingly honest and raw. Amidst the coming to terms with one's body in relation to another are moments which allude to the more difficult parts of a relationship. From 'Miel'

> You will know what to eat
> You will know where honey is
> And I do not know how to find honey without you.
> I alone without you

And from 'Cocoon'

> It's not... meant to be a strife...
> it's not ... meant to be... a struggle up hill.

Can I ever know this person? Am I so forever changed from our being together? Honestly, I hope so.

When all aclash over my refusal to deal with some aspect of being an adult, how can we untangle ourselves, untangle our love and identities from the practical matter of getting on with our lives?

The silent difficulty of being at the bar with my girlfriend instead of the usual alone. The best bartender, playing Beach House which I'd never pick on my own but am overjoyed to hear, making feeling obligated to not wear headphones (lest I be incredibly rude) more survivable. She's reading *Portrait of a Lady*, a terribly long thing I'm only kind of glad to have slogged through a decade or two ago, while the author's *Turn of the Screw*, seemingly a legitimate influence on this project, sits like a tumor in the back of my mind with its obfuscations, lost-to-time innuendoes, and tortured storytelling affectations. Everything's quasi – the basketball games are all semi-relevant, the hockey game is the same (0-7 makes performing the final third hardly worth keeping the rink frozen).

She's in spots: a polka dot blouse a bit unbuttoned (she asked this morn if letting a button remain unsutured suited the outfit and I said yes) and the beak and eye of the bird tattooed on her chest is peeking out. I joked early on in our relationship that should someone ask why she had that hummingbird inkilly hovering there she should lie and say something about seeing a hummingbird the day her mother or grandmother died or somesuch. Her real reason lacks poetry, romance. Actually, it lacks much of anything – and as I remember this the extent to which she will forever be a cypher rears its head and frightens me as much as it ever has – as she chose this and all of her tattoos as far as I've been able to tell at random, or based on minimally considered aesthetic principles – strange from someone with so certain an eye, so discerning. A random mark, symbolizing a willingness to be marked, an artificial kinship with those who've been marked thusly. But not really – how can a flower or bird ensconced on the skin, however permanently, be the same as a similar sketch produced post-trauma, post-partum, in-memoriam? The pain and the permanence are shared. Decisiveness for decisiveness's sake is no less resolute.

I'm tattooless, the one piercing I had (mall-done, top of my left ear [*I had to reach up to feel the scar to remember what side*] long since closed).

> He says, "Why are you bare?
> Bare as the day
> day you were borne from your mother?"
>
> I say, "So you can tattoo me
> with the marks of a lover."[64]

Nothing so romantic drives my avoidance of further modifications; rather something private - a fear of needles, a recognition that the certainty which drove me in my teens and twenties and thirties wasn't the end of the story, that I'd need to develop some more indecision, an ability to listen, a willingness to feel regret, to atone.

I'll admit the obvious – the suggestion of a kind of darker side is a draw, regardless of whether it ever show its face. A penchant or resilience for pain, an instinct to mark in blood and ink significant experiences and memories and loves is attractive (though I've not chosen to do so myself) Funny how knowing that she's done this with none of these imperatives didn't subtract from the incredibleness which tied me inextricably to the girl.

One day: tattoos together. *What-ever.* In italics. Or some other in-joke.

---

[64] From the Diane Cluck song "Ink and Needles" off her self-titled album.

I entered the train station with a magnetic whiff of a
ticket – the Clipper card in my wallet sits in hibernation
until placed, wallet and all, against the plastic circle on the
gate, the machine calls out, elicits from my card an
inventory, takes its toll, leaves me a little (virtually)
lighter in the pocket book.

A woman sat next to me on the train, relaxed at first.
Soon she was searching her pockets for something,
fumbling with her keys, then on her knees looking
beneath the seat for something. She looked genuinely
startled – something was missing, something important.
And this something was here, somewhere. I was recruited
in the effort; her purse was turned inside out, pockets re-
checked, we lifted the actual seat revealing a jangle of
rusted springs, little spills of morning coffee or evening
beer feeding their soft decline. I had no idea how to
console her – losing things is such a failure, makes one
doubt the continuity of consciousness, the persistence of
matter, the arrow of time (if you let it). She was both
pleading and helpless while trying to seem stoic, self-
sufficient. She left the train unsatisfied.

In a bar, when here to get things done, I view strangers
with a certain malice, especially should their appearance
or voice cause them to stand out so much as to make
ignoring their presence un-ignorable. Not that people
should be invisible, rather that I hope to retain the ability
to tune into and out of the world around me. Some noise

is great; watching the goings on in the bar is important, saves me from myself.

I'm in that booth again – a group of guys has the other half, is eating a pizza, drinking a pitcher, and suffering a game of dominos which two of the participants are completely ill prepared for, the third thinks he is teaching the others but has the game all wrong. Still, they're having fun if a bit painedly so.

A memory: having said a terrible thing about a person a guilty disappointment when, confronted with the object of my adolescent outburst, I can see that they don't know what I've said. I know they couldn't've heard from a mutual acquaintance what I've said yet I'm surprised, face to face, that even without being directly told of my idiocy my guilt doesn't immediately tell all. That phrase '____'s ears must be ringing' springs to mind. Because they should be - what has been said is so excess of what is just and fair given the circumstances and social norms that the surplus cruelty should've slipped paranormally across time and space alerting this person to my childishness, their unfair treatment.

On TV: sports done, each TV has random programing streaming. One has the elaborate, by hand refresh of the bed of a truck's understructure: rust is ground off, parts are replaced, eventually the vehicle is rebuilt with newly refreshed bones. On another, the scene is meant to establish the interviewee as a photographer. The darkroom experience is a bit too light; this look (dim, red-lit, pictures hung by clothespins on twine) is maintained in the middle distance though those interviewed are bathed in full spectrum. The elemental alchemy of black and white photography exists as a narrative device/trope, completely removed from the audience's lived experience but not without value. Think of the relevance description-wise of asking someone to Xerox something – the machine/chemical process may differ but the specter of the original remains, colors one's perspective on the act.

6. Interspecific plums

a.

The best and worst part of a relationship are the seams,
the gaps between which become apparent now and then
despite any effort to keep them mudded over. Seams and
gaps... these are not the same. A seam conjoins two,
attempts via its art to appear seam-less. Where as a gap
has never been so close –though it may have, due to
clever navigation and cartography, seemed hidden,
forgotten, irrelevant.

A break – some gap in communication, some distraction
of one or both parties causes a misfire and then a sudden
slip, like plates in a quake, blossoms into brash, brief, not
ignorable existence.

What sutures? What forges a safe path amidst a field that
may appear even and infinite with ice and snow but
conceals amidst all that even whiteness crevasses –
inescapable; we're falling, scraping against walls foothold-
less but craggy enough to catch and tear at flesh.

What'll we do, goals met because we set them very low,
day long since retired and the phases of night with which
we're familiar (never ones for post-witching hour forays –
these were threatened early on maybe and occasionally
one of us dragged the other into wee hours; lately lateness
has been firmly off the table) shed leaving us unmoored
in the increasingly unfamiliar crease which enfolds today-
yesterday-tomorrow?

I'm glad for this uncertainty – noone'll ask us for shit besides our cat's insistence on something not quite communicable via mews, pawings at, wistful stares into the void etc. The two of us, satisfied with whatever next episode streams, entwining attention at the plot (is this a standalone or relevant long-term?), a slight dozing-off, and an occasional notice that next to us is a body, warm and masseous.

b.

A pluot seems comfortable being neither here nor there. Not yet settled enough into language (though so familiar) as to reside on the page without a swiggly red underline, the fruit itself asks little – eat me or don't. Really, who finds either of its parent objectionable? Pluots are also known as interspecific plums, Pluots®, apriums, apriplums, or plumcots. We both love a good portmanteau.

The contortions one goes to make a stretch words not repetitive sometimes of Achene – "a type of simple dry fruit also sometimes called akene and occasionally achenium or achenocarp" – is conjured should one look for a synonym to fruit.[65] Rosehips, the fruit of cannabis, the seeds of maple... accurate as these are taxidermically fruit but really it is an unlikely confluence of words that finds a reference for bananas, apples, peaches easily exchangeable for such hard, bitter things. Fecund, yes,

---

[65] From the wiki, as one might have guessed

but theirs feels so much less apparent on the face of it. Eating a dusty green-skinned plum or pluot called a 'flavor queen' that this thing is of life and has within the seed for ever more life is not hard to conjure. A fleshy mess, pit gripped protected at its core, this flesh is nothing more than a ploy inciting animals to swallow and later defecate the seed further away from the tree than the law of gravity and whims of weather would accomplish (echoing the sweetness of the preceding flower from which the fruit sprang being itself a ploy for pollinators).

The smell of electrical fire, acrid and precise. Current rolling through a system meets an impediment – the throughput of a given juncture is insufficient to handle the flow; a wire is frayed, the wrong parts have been used, more power than can be handled has been let in. Gasses ignite at the overworked intersection, atoms all excited and aglow. How quickly this odor pervades, and so unmistakably nothing else! Staring at a black box with a few blinking lights but little else to indicate its function and/or health, a single whiff of this charged air is enough to indicate 'danger!'. You turn it off and on again, you unplug it, you begin to reconcile it's days as numbered while holding onto hope that the fault can be sussed out, repaired, worked around.

Thought – Colors exist on a spectrum, such a literal thing, every color can be parsed based on multiple systems (r-g-b, c-m-k-y etc.) and be remade or at least approximated. All light can also be broken down, it's constituent colors directly related to the periodic table's growing list. Surely the same must exist for smell. To smell is to take in particles which interact with sensory cells in the nose. Sound requires some substance to propagate through, color is the trace of some substance emitting or reflecting light. Smell is direct, like taste it is a direct contact with a foreign substance. If you can smell food, some of it is already inside you prior to taking a bite.

This strange smell – some of the tiny fire's smoke has registered within. Seemingly post-industrial, perhaps there is something of lightening's burn through the air on its journey from sky to earth which meant something at one time, a deep memory referenced by this precious acridity.

8. Fragment

The primal scene: the fantasy of witnessing one's own conception. Like a reverse ghost produced beyond the border of birth rather than that of expiry, haunting the world, marked by the knowledge gained by this atemporal haunt. Were one to make the lights flicker, the sound of rattling chains, a wolf's howl, or to produce a gust of wind despite one's parents having closed tight the windows and doors for privacy...

8. A human pearl

<u>a.</u>

> The doors flew open, and I was ushered into a
> saloon curiously full of pale light, which did not
> culminate on any spot, nor proceed from any centre,
> nor flicker with any motion of the air, but filled
> every nook and corner, making all things deliciously
> distinct; different from our light of gas or candle, as
> is the difference between a clear southern
> atmosphere and that of our misty England.
> *-unsure?*

This 'ghostly' light is curiously similar to modern electric
lighting, especially as provided by fluorescent tubes. Or
like the sun sitting somewhere behind an even blanket of
cloud. It's with no astronomical guide to my place upon
the sphere of Earth that I find myself not quite able to
proceed, troubled.

b.

A band of under-twenties is playing something
mistakable for heartfelt jazz at the bar. Usually confining
themselves to mellow standards and covers of pop tunes
(that easy pleasure of the moment of recognition — it's
The Cure, it's "Superstition"), for this song they've
drifted into some more challenging Miles Davis territory,
they're getting kinda free with it. Afraid of offending
anyone my headphones are off, at least until they finish
this set. My beer is cold on this reasonable facsimile of an

Indian summer evening. Everything seems a version, pastiche.

Like a bargain Kubrick: from this other booth I look out onto a large flat screen TV, a relatively recent addition to the bar, sitting power-off, black save a tiny red dot in the bottom left corner – tiny, bright, and direct as a laser. Between my seat and the TV above, a series of three Edison bulbs, slightly off-kilter, filaments ablaze. They are reflected in the black glass – the further away the light (closer to me) the larger the strange halo the reflected bulb casts in the screen. I'm stuck with these sensations outside me, and within, unable to focus on the imaginary.

There is something. Sitting betwixt pinky and the finger next to it. Underneath the skin.

And I can't help but obsess on this thing beneath my skin. I looked it up: excoriation (or *dermatillomania* and several less official-sounding terms) — the repeated urge to pick at one's own skin to the point that damage is caused. I've most certainly this, relatively under control but here, with this thing, too hot, over-jazzed...

A cursory search nets nothing: I couldn't find a word for the pleasure felt when fluid is pressed out of one's body. An abscess, acne, a spider bite... all give a certain pleasure.

It is not unlike a small ball bearing, right there at the knuckle. Loose, affixed neither to the skin or whatever lies beneath at that juncture. A human pearl.

And, a moment of intense pain where just recently there was simply dread and wonder, it bursts out, this foreign body is free, my hand is bloody, the pain is numbed by wonder. Hard like a ball of opaque white glass, yet undulating in its way, subtly writhing.

c.

Worm, pupae or grub-like, a creamy semi-translucent outer shell which may be either wet or simply glossy, it writhes as much due to interior goings on as any sort of attempted locomotion. There are patches of thin, glassy white hairs jutting out from its rock hard exterior. Or rather, there are bands of them, invisible mostly, especially apparent only when backlit like the subtle fur of a partner's forehead viewable in the morning sun. One orifice, barely noticeable when not in use as a small dimple on one end of the thing; when operating it fits so snug against whatever comes in or out as to deny a peek inside. It is an entrance only – whatever is ingested is fully integrated by the thing; it gains mass in kind. The only wavering is due to some kind of breathing or other exchange of gasses, presumably occurring on the surface area of the fine hairs. Limbless, it is only through preserving the impenetrability of its exterior that it achieves a modicum of security, keeps hidden its interior.

Dissecting the creature post-mortem is done with great difficulty as its surface is indifferent to a common scalpel or saw; the most clean work has thus far been done with a diamond coated blade at a high rpm though tests are ongoing with laser systems, initially thought to do too much damage to be of use. Therein reside several limbs, not dramatically inhuman, complete with multiple joints (maybe a few more points of articulation than your or my arm) and culminating in quite natural-seeming hands, fingernails and all. These nails seem to know how long to be as it is hard to imagine a system having evolved to trim them though now one could imagine some metal implement being interred into the thing, used, and then excreted (a little wetter for the experience). Its complex of organs is not unfamiliar – not surprising as dog, snake, eagle, elephant all manage to have generally the same innards – but the arrangement is peculiar. No two of the things have an identical organization of structures. Indeed, were one to scan a cluster of these creatures the placement and quantity of each's livers, kidneys, hearts, lungs (ed.- lungs fed through pores at the end of the aforementioned hairs), one could use a map of these parts as a kind of fingerprint with which to distinguish individuals.

What few specimens have been vivisected have revealed at the ends of the hand traditional fingerprints, however they are not useful in identifying each as the interior skin is constantly subject to varying degrees of moisture; more often than not the surprisingly leather-like interior dermis is pruned-up, rumpled skin patterns twisted beyond recognition, dried (somehow) and then wrinkled again. Post-mortem perhaps, with the right combination of dedication and motivation one could brave the odor of the inside of the worm once the body is broken into and delicately unfurl each digit's skin and register usable prints but in practice MRI or other scanning techniques done on living or recently deceases creatures are enough to catalogue specimens that are externally identical.

Reproduction is achieved by a method completely unique – the hairs each wear on their exterior a variant of the creatures DNA in a distinct knot, surrounded by a complex of simple machine-like protein structures. Brushing against one of the creatures the hairs imperceptibly slough off these 'seeds'. Their surface proteins drive the things inward, sacrificing themselves in the process and slowly leaving bare the core. Should chance and the action of its shell grant it purchase on the nucleus of a host's cell, it latch on to the core DNA not unlike a virus, not duplicating *itself* but rather performing a score, a dance of cuts and edits in the host's DNA.

In the human genome there is a tremendous amount of junk DNA, DNA that doesn't code for proteins. Estimates for the biologically functional fraction of our genome based on comparative genomics range between 8 and 15%. These seeds combine their own sequence with portions lying dormant within the host's to form a healthy, dividing individual cell. The host cell recognizes this intruder, an immune response is but the newly born thing quickly blasticizes doubly – at an early sixteen-cell stage an inner void is formed to create a typical blastula; at this distinct point (the exact timing mechanism and process of triadic division is unknown) each cell's division undergoes a seven-percent chance of tripletting, the atypical third cell is sent inward forming a core which itself creates a second blastocyst. The outer shell of cells is unique in nature as it presents itself as natural enough as to not shock the host system into annihilating it but strange enough to attract t-cells with which it builds a micro womb of sorts, the thing floating in a carefully balanced suppuration.

Three or so days after implantation the host typically feels something going on at the contact site, a deep, semi-hard point. Eventually the host will attempt to evacuate the region; incredibly the thing's only survival potential is if this is done in such a way as to find itself in a body of water, washed into the sewer system, disposed of in a lake etc. But even this is not simple – the thing is extraordinarily hard and resilient, capable of remaining dormant in dry conditions for potentially years before finding its way into a body of water. Indeed, patience and resilience are its key tools. Finding a dark nook in an estuary, one will slowly grow itself for years, taking in almost any organic mater as food, processing it in its peculiar viscera.

It has been suggested that these strange grub-like 'adults' – ranging in size from a marble to a fully-grown man – are merely the adolescence of something stranger still.

There is anecdotal evidence supporting this hypothesis. One young man found a rather large specimen in a river on the lee side of a boulder. Wading in to the outcropping, he managed to take a photo of the thing and to open up a video chat with a friend. The friend describes how the man set his phone down to examine the thing which was looser than usual, more opalescent (the initial photo confirms this). At this point he heard screams intermingled with rough to make out narration as to what was happening. He describes the thing tearing open down its length, its inside arms grabbing at him, slashing at him. The whole seemed to be folding in on itself, flipping inside out though how this could work with its organs all splayed on the newly formed outside of the thing is hard to imagine. The recording is tough to listen to; his screams are muffled by what must be the two of them splashing violently, and periods in which the man is presumably taken beneath the surface, only to reemerge, regain his breath, and scream again.

The man was never found, nothing of him, not his body or his clothes though the phone remained where he lay it, slowly draining its battery. Nothing was found of the thing either, though a subsequent detailed search of the river downstream uncovered what may have been a few of its perfectly manicured fingernails, found clinging to a bank of algae.

9. Exit

As if my bones've fused; why else do my missives to muscles fail to stir limbs? I can look down across my blanketed form at my body, laid haphazardly before me. Why won't it stir, not a twitch, my breath (assuming still pulsing) not enough to press the covers noticeably upward. Even my eyelids resist — I'd love to close my eyes tight and scream inwardly "*WAKE UP*" or, alternatively, "GO BACK TO SLEEP," but alas they refuse. Only changes the bit of dawn light easing from tone to tone across it all, the temperature gradually rising...

That thing: like a word read but never said: *exeunt.*